Nicholas Michell

Sibyl of Cornwall

A Poetic Tale

Nicholas Michell

Sibyl of Cornwall
A Poetic Tale

ISBN/EAN: 9783744713061

Printed in Europe, USA, Canada, Australia, Japan

Cover: Foto ©Thomas Meinert / pixelio.de

More available books at **www.hansebooks.com**

SIBYL OF CORNWALL.

A Poetical Tale.

THE LAND'S END, ST. MICHAEL'S MOUNT,

AND

OTHER POEMS.

BY

NICHOLAS MICHELL,

AUTHOR OF

"RUINS OF MANY LANDS," "PLEASURE," "THE POETRY OF CREATION," &c.

LONDON:

CHAPMAN AND HALL, 193, PICCADILLY.

1869.

TO

THE MEMORY OF

SIR HUMPHRY DAVY, BARONET,

LATE OF PENZANCE, CORNWALL;

A MAN DISTINGUISHED BY REFINED TASTE,.

BUT MORE CELEBRATED FOR HIS DISCOVERIES
IN CHEMICAL SCIENCE;

THESE PAGES

ARE

INSCRIBED

BY

HIS COUNTRYMAN AND RELATIVE,

THE AUTHOR.

CONTENTS.

SIBYL OF CORNWALL.

PART I. TO PART XV. . . . . Page 1 *to* 140

MISCELLANEOUS POEMS.

	PAGE
THE LAND'S END	143
ST. MICHAEL'S MOUNT	147
THE SEASON OF YOUTH	151
THE EVENING OF LIFE	155
THE DREAM OF THE LONDON SEAMSTRESS	157
WOMAN'S LOVE	160
HYMN TO THE RISING SUN	163
OCEAN'S CHANGES	166
FRENCH AND ENGLISH BEAUTIES	169

CONTENTS.

<table>
<tr><td></td><td align="right">PAGE</td></tr>
<tr><td>Solitary Confinement</td><td align="right">172</td></tr>
<tr><td>The Vagrant's Child</td><td align="right">175</td></tr>
<tr><td>The Classic Rhone</td><td align="right">178</td></tr>
<tr><td>Woman's Modern Aspirations</td><td align="right">180</td></tr>
<tr><td>Morning on Ramsgate Sands</td><td align="right">183</td></tr>
<tr><td>The Echo in the Vale</td><td align="right">185</td></tr>
<tr><td>The Meeting of the Lovers</td><td align="right">186</td></tr>
<tr><td>The Present Hour</td><td align="right">188</td></tr>
<tr><td>The Burial of a Young Officer at Sea</td><td align="right">191</td></tr>
<tr><td>The Beautiful Lady</td><td align="right">194</td></tr>
<tr><td>The Old Church Porch</td><td align="right">196</td></tr>
<tr><td>Rest</td><td align="right">198</td></tr>
<tr><td>The Convalescent</td><td align="right">200</td></tr>
<tr><td>Dreaming of Paradise</td><td align="right">202</td></tr>
<tr><td>Far at Sea</td><td align="right">205</td></tr>
<tr><td>The Burning Emigrant Ship</td><td align="right">207</td></tr>
<tr><td>The Lily of Eden</td><td align="right">213</td></tr>
<tr><td>Beautiful Things</td><td align="right">215</td></tr>
<tr><td>Progress</td><td align="right">217</td></tr>
<tr><td>The Ray of Light</td><td align="right">219</td></tr>
<tr><td>Oriental Beauty</td><td align="right">222</td></tr>
<tr><td>The Dying Flower Girl</td><td align="right">224</td></tr>
<tr><td>Past and Future</td><td align="right">226</td></tr>
</table>

PAGE

A Cornish Village 228

The Lovliest Thing on Earth 232

Spirits Everywhere 234

The Guardian Angel and Child 236

Evening at Hastings 238

To-Morrow 241

The Widow and the Portrait 244

The Blind Girl 246

The Fountain of the Sweet and Bitter . . . 248

The Cry of the Unresigned 250

The Loved and Lost 252

Mylor Church and Falmouth Harbour . . . 255

The Waking Infant 259

Spare Her, Death! 261

The Maid of the Isles 263

The Young Opera Dancer 265

The Military Hero 268

Night on the Cornish Coast 270

Early Morning in Regent's Park 272

The Tower of London 275

The Mystery of Music 279

Summer is Come 281

The Spirit of Ruin 283

CONTENTS.

PAGE

A Reverie among the Alps 286

Nature's Morning Hymn of Praise 288

Katherine Southey, In Memoriam 290

Mourn Not. 292

———

Short Poems designed for Music . . page 295 *to* 308

ADDRESS TO CORNWALL.

Cornubia, hail! thou land of mist and cloud,
  Along whose coasts the hurrying tempests blow
Their deep-mouthed trumpets, while, like warriors proud,
  On mighty rocks, the billows charging go.
Land of the granite peak, so wild, so bare,
Great Nature looks a ragged beggar there;
Yet, stored beneath thy soil, rich coffers lie,
And wealth untold those dreary vaults supply.

Despite thy gloom and storms, oft smiles most bright
  Flash on thy shores from sunniest, bluest skies;
Peace after passion, after darkness light,
  And after tears, sweet Beauty's laughing eyes.

B

The rainbow sits in glory on thy hills,
With dewy wine her bowl the kingcup fills;
Soft airs blow fragrance from the daisied vale,
Where brooks sing lyrics to the throstle's tale.

O yes, the wild Land's End, Tintagel's rocks,
   May war for ever with the sounding deep;
Granite-ribbed mountains brave the tempest's shocks,
   And the drear Mines in long, long deserts sweep;
Yet nooks adorn rough Cornwall, sweet and blest—
So gems will grace the dusky Ethiop's breast—
Plains where fertility each blessing showers,
Glens where Arcadia smiles in fruits and flowers.

Behold bright Tamar, England's Arno, sparkling
   By groves and meads, by rocks with moss
     embrown'd;
See Fowey crystal-trailing, flashing, darkling,
   While Lynher dances on with joyous bound:
Clear-bosomed Fal divides the winding steeps,
Woods fringe its course, the church-tower mirror'd
     sleeps;
Beauty in greenest coves doth laughing hide,
Peace, like an angel, watching by its tide.

With glittering rocks the Lizard breasts the waves,
  Emerald and flame, beyond art's painting grand!*
Sure sea-nymphs fashioned Kynance' wondrous caves,
  Roofed with rich glory by their cunning hand.
Mount of St. Michael! did that hallowed steep
Drop from some lovelier star, to grace our deep?
So strange, so beautiful, it seems to stand,
Half in the clasping ocean, half on land.†

Cornwall, no more the barbarous wrecker hails
  The stranded ship, and plies his robber-trade;
But honesty and kindness walk thy vales,
  And art and science there bright homes have made.

---

* The beautiful stone, called Serpentine, abounds at the Lizard Point—a stone, for the most part, of a deep green colour, veined with scarlet. Kynance Cove, in the neighbourhood, is considered one of the most extraordinary spots on our western coasts. Here also the rocks are composed of the rare and gorgeous marble above named.

† St. Michael's Mount, near Penzance, renowned in early religious history, is separated from the mainland twice a-day, by the flowing of the tide. This famous rock-pyramid of nature's formation, rising to the height of more than 200 feet, and crowned with its ancient monastic building, presents in itself a strikingly picturesque object; while the surrounding scenery possesses a beauty and a magnificence, that cannot fail to captivate the imagination.

Proud, loyal are thy sons, and many a name
Sheds on thy cairn-crowned hills the light of fame;
Davy and Opie, stars unfading, shine,
And while they flash their lustre, heighten thine.

SIBYL OF CORNWALL.

PART I.

Day slowly to his ocean-couch retires,
　　Warm with his travel o'er heaven's sultry plains;
His eye is languid, shooting softened fires;
　　Around, above, the soul of stillness reigns.
The western sky is like a mighty rose,
The clouds, the leaves, upfolding in repose,
And, as they fold, more deeply red they turn,
Till all the broad horizon seems to burn.

The stream forgets its blueness, crimson glowing,
　　The trees, late green, in hoods of saffron shine,
Each little gadding rill in blushes flowing,
　　As if by magic turned to ruby wine.
The cairn, the brake, each flower that scents the way,
All catch the tints flung back by dreamy day;
Awhile on Nature, dropp'd from burnished skies,
A gorgeous robe, half fire, half colour, lies.

O'er level ocean broods the dove of peace;
　At evening hour do angel-forms descend,
And by their presence make all discords cease,
　And their own beauty to earth's beauty lend?
Ships move like spirits o'er the placid billow,
That swells or falls—an amber, shining pillow;
Along the coast the sea-voice floats on air,
Like murmur in the shell, or whispered prayer.

High up a glen that opened to the sea,
　A granite mansion decked the sloping hill;
Its rugged walls spoke hoar antiquity,
　Though comfort, beauty, lingered round it still.
Old were the casements, and the roof was steep;
In front, white statues seemed calm watch to keep;
Behind rose patriarch elm-trees, tall and grey,
Rooks cawing round their tops the live-long day.

Hedged with green hollies, looking o'er the wave,
　Inviting to deep thought and soft repose,
A garden spread its sweets; the wild bee gave
　His heart to riot up; the bashful rose,
Prevailed on by the sun, expanded there
Her fragrant bosom to the loving air;
And many a flower, of many a beauteous dye,
Peeped from the earth to laugh upon the sky.

But floored with spars, by tangled shrubs o'ergrown,
  A rustic arbour shunned the prying view—
As fair a nook as love e'er made his own,
  Or fancy asks, when love and life are new.
Not ours to paint a weird Calypso's grot,
Though still Ulysses, in such magic spot,
Might linger long, forget the stormy wave,
Worship bewitching eyes, and bow a slave.

Sunset now washed with softest glossy gold,
  The ancient mansion, flowers, and turf of green,
And strove, with eager ray, like robber bold,
  To force an entrance thro' that arbour's screen;
But the thick leaves the level shafts repelled,
Save when a straggling beam the eye beheld,
Piercing the verdant gloom with quivering fire,
And running through the stems, like golden wire.

Ye enter—are the wild birds nestling here,
  Or fairies gathering for their evening dance?
No speckled throats or fluttering wings appear,
  No elfin warrior shakes his rush-green lance;
But one of human mould, with eyes of light,
And lovely as a sylphid, meets the sight,
Combining all the ideal's gorgeous dreams,
With all the warmth of beauty's living beams.

A deep voluptuous calmness held the spot;
　　Ye heard the faintest air that kiss'd the trees,
The peasant's laughter from the distant cot,
　　The drowsy hum of home-returning bees;
The billows, breaking on the broad flat shore,
Just shook the pebbles, and forgot to roar,
Their murmurs, bidding harsher thoughts depart,
Rising so softly from great Ocean's heart.

She leant upon her hand; before her lay
　　An open book; but those deep museful eyes
From the late thralling page were turned away,
　　And through the arbour's entrance sought the skies.
A something calms the spirit, holy, blest,
That all have felt when watching the red west;
The clouds of glory lift the soul, that seems
Nearer to heaven, and borne away in dreams.

Sibyl was gazing motionless and hushed;
　　Her bosom, heaving gently, as in sleep,
Told only that she breathed; upon her rushed
　　A current of old memories, strong and deep:
As her eye followed slow the floating mass
Of cloudy splendour, fancy seemed to pass
Along those opal battlements, and rise,
Step after step, to God's bright paradise.

Not common was her beauty; in warm Spain,
  Or southern Italy, or those bright isles
Whose marble cliffs gleam o'er the Ægean main,
  Fair beings, like that maid, may shed their smiles :
A sorcery dwelleth in such forms, to sway
All who may gaze—hearts struggle, yet obey ;
Creatures, once seen, whate'er the strong endeavour,
They haunt men's souls, and memory's world for ever.

She leant upon her hand—unchecked, unbound,
  Fell from her stooping head a cloud of tresses,
In Nature's sweet profusion, wreathing round
  Her arms, her shoulders, with their wild caresses.
Those locks were deepest chesnut, and they beamed
With glossy light, when sunshine on them streamed,
Well suited to her features' changeful play,
Where never night was seen, but always day.

Her cheek no roses tinted, but its brown
  Was soft and glowing as a sunset-heaven,
And witched with dimples; her high brow looked down,
  As if her soul some conscious power were given :
And yet there seemed a sweetness in her pride,
A gushing forth of feeling nought could hide ;
The mind and heart might oft at variance be,
But heart, warm struggler, won the victory.

Her eyes resembled not those eyes which beam,
   The windows of a gentle soul that looks
All timid forth, where mild emotions gleam,
   Plainly as pebbles shining in the brooks;
Nor those that never flash ambition's ray,
But from the great and glorious turn away—
Turn from the stars, the ocean in its power,
More pleased to view a rill, or mark a flower.

Hers, mirror of strong character, were seen,
   Black in their liquid beauty, with a light
That, did not longest lashes form a screen,
   Had blazed too fiercely warm, too wildly bright:
Yet nought unfeminine, ungentle, shone
In those dark orbs, by feeling lit alone,
As Nature formed them large and lustrous too,
To match the soul, and all that sparkled through.

Then purity, like moonlight, glowed around her,
   And modesty, and sweetest maiden grace,
Defence more strong than breastplate, closely bound her;
   Her form was chastely beauteous as her face:
Beholders might be ravished; but her air,
Her brilliant presence, like some magic there,
Repelled the forward, till the base might feel
The power of virtue, and to goodness kneel.

Sibyl had móved no limb, but now her gaze
  Dropped from the western glory ; she was blind
To all without—within, thought turned its rays,
  And she was looking, but with eyes of mind.
A distant scene enthralled her ; strange the power
Fancy exerts in reason's waking hour,
Bearing away the soul o'er vale and hill,
And yet that soul the body's prisoner still.

Bright in the sun a mighty river flowed,
  The banks adorned with plane and spreading palm ;
White tents stood round, hot skies like metal glowed,
  All things seemed basking in the sultry calm :
Nought stirred amid the resting soldier ranks,
The elephant was slumbering on the banks ;
Deep drowsy stillness hushed the earth, the air, .
As if no breathing host—the dead lay there.

He sat beside the ancient Indian stream,
  And watched it flow, to saddened thought resigned ;
Oh, did he think, in that absorbing dream,
  Of English shores, and her he left behind ?
Or dreamt he of a future crowned with fame,
A hero's bays to grace his youthful name ?
Was he in spirit 'mid the fearful fray,
The happy past from memory swept away ?

No, she believed that he, her early love,
    Would not forget her in that far-off land ;
Faith, changeless, fixed, as golden stars above,
    Burned in her breast, while time affection fanned.
Thus did the eyes of soul behold him there,
Doubt of his truth awoke no anxious care.
Yes, he did think of her, that tranquil hour,
His Cornish maiden, in her distant bower.

They loved, when scarce the meaning of that word
    Dawned on their youthful minds; life's hours had past
On rough Cornubia's shores, their bosoms stirred
    By the same spells wild Nature round them cast :
Union of tastes another union wove,
Love for the glorious woke another love ;
And, growing one in spirit, one in heart,
Each of the other's being seemed a part.

'Twas in this garden they had sighed farewell,
    On such an eve of beauty.   Sibyl's fears
Blanched her young cheek, grief's rain in torrents fell ;
    But he breathed hope, and kissed away her tears.
Pledges of endless truth by both were given,
Each lived for each, they placed their trust in heaven ;
Though years might sever them, as seas would part,
What can divide fond heart in thought from heart ?

But see where bright the garden fountain plays,
   Dropping on shells beneath with murmurs low,
A man sedately paces, evening's rays
   Falling across his path with quivering glow.
His mien is dignified, yet gentle now;
Thought, placid as the landscape, smooths his brow.
A country pastor he, whose feet have trod
Scenes that to him, the preacher, preach of God.

How happy glides the calm-soul'd pastor's life,
   In some green rural district, far away
From anxious cities, mad ambition's strife,
   His sweetest toil 'mid Nature's haunts to stray!
His sweetest toil to drink pure learning's stream,
To shed on darkened mind instruction's beam;
To heal the soul diseased, point out the snare
By folly set, and soothe the poor man's care.

Trelawn seemed living but for others' weal,
   A rampart round the weak his goodness reared;
What others felt, his heart would ever feel,
   Virtue high raised him, charity endeared;
Malice stung not, e'en envy was disarmed;
Strangers, who came to blame, still left him charmed;
Harsh men would kindly looks upon him cast,
And village mothers bless'd him as he past.

A well of joy to him was learning's page,
    Grecian and Roman lore a banquet spread;
While astronomic wonders could engage
    A mind from which all narrow feelings fled:
And thus life's peaceful road the pastor trod,
Loving his simple flock, his child, his God;
No wish to soar, devout contentment given,
Finding joy here, and hoping joy in heaven.

Yet while, glass-smooth, the current seemed to flow,
    Trelawn of late was changed; some deep distress
Oppressed his soul, a stranger once to woe;
    What gave delight, no longer now could bless:
Something untold lay heavy at his heart;
And he would absent sit, and ofttimes start,
Wander for hours beside the cliff-bound deep,
Toss on his couch, and mutter in his sleep.

As now, by that bright fount, the muser paced,
    His late calm look departed; sorrow threw
A shadow on his soul. He stopped, and faced
    The gorgeous west, where day bade earth adieu.
Sadly his vision rested on the globe,
The everlasting sun-god, in a robe
Of saffron clouds, his golden wings unfurled,
A living glory fading from the world.

But Nature's splendour failed to yield him peace ;
  He gazed upon the rising, splashing fount,
Whose jets, like restless fancies, would not cease ;
  Each diamond wave his eye appeared to count ;
And then he conned his Greek, and thought how long
The nations had been charmed with Homer's song ;
But vain the attempt to lull dark dreams to rest,
Or draw the barb that rankled in his breast.

He sat upon a rustic bench, and there
  Bowed his lined forehead on his shrunken hand ;
The last beams trembled on his thin, white hair ;
  What could affect him ? why so crush'd, unmann'd ?
He whom all loved—of other men the guide—
Who, though he gave, had all his wants supplied—
Faultless before the world—the pure, severe ;
And yet he shivered, as from guilt or fear.

A step—he raised his head, beheld his child ;
  Perplexed she stood before him ; for her eyes
Had seen the grief, whose gusts came oft and wild ;
  Her shrinking ear had caught his secret sighs.
She took his hand ; she kissed his hueless cheek,
And gazed into his face, but did not speak ;
Then gently sat beside him, while she strove
To read his thoughts, and soothe him with her love.

But e'en her efforts could not charm away
   Mind's heavy burden; to her fond appeal
He made no answer; deep his secret lay,
   And what he felt, his soul alone would feel.
Though prayers and kisses brought a softness o'er
The father's heart, that heart seemed wrung the more;
Gazing to heaven, a few slow tears he shed,
Looked silent thanks, and drooped again his head.

But twilight's arms were now 'round Nature thrown,
   Shadows on tree and meadow greyly fell;
The billows crept on shore with fainter tone,
   The linnet ceased his vespers in the dell.
A hush came down upon the world, and gave,
Without its gloom, the quiet of the grave;
And lovely one small star flashed out on high,
Like some bright guardian angel's opening eye.

Trelawn beheld the scene; it touched his soul:
   " God grant me strength—forgive me, righteous
      heaven !"
He rose, and seemed strong feeling to control,
   And sought the porch, his hand to Sibyl given.
" 'Tis past," he cried; " my heart is tranquil now !"
His limbs no longer trembled; on his brow
No more hung fear-drops; gloom to light gave place,
And placid smiles illumed the pastor's face.

SIBYL OF CORNWALL.

PART II.

Brightly and cheerily the morning rose,
  Sprinkling soft amber rays o'er all the deep;
Nature's wide realms were freshened by repose,
  And cape and cove flung off their dreamy sleep;
The towering cliffs looked out to greet the sun,
The billow's trumpet sounded—day begun!
In open seas great barks pursued their way,
And little skiffs shot jocund o'er the bay.

On land the birds were all astir, and winging
  From blossom'd bough to bough; the mottled
    thrush
In the deep thicket to his true love singing,
  His melody one steady, flute-like gush;
While on spread plumes, quick winnowing in the sky,
Upwheeling and upwheeling, still more high,
As if his spirit scorned earth's lowlier sod,
The lark, at heaven's gemmed gate, sang hymns to
    God.

Morn flushed the happy face of all the skies;
  The waking flowers were busy sending up
Their prayers in odours, spreading their rich dyes,
  And offering to the bees the honied cup.
Curled from the cottage chimney silvery smoke,
Sharp, lively voices from the hamlet broke;
And soon the plough went winding o'er the soil,
And peasants, light of heart, commenced their toil.

She tripped along the honeysuckled lane,
  Sweet as the odorous morning, and as gay,
Fresh as the breeze, in-wafted from the main,
  And with a low-humm'd tune beguiled the way.
Her hat but half concealed her chesnut hair;
For summer warmth, her graceful throat was bare;
Her little feet, e'en as a song-bird's light,
Were scarcely seen beneath her dress of white.

The pastor's daughter bore upon her arm,
  Pomona-like, a basket, stored with grapes,
And medicine for the sick; that sight might charm
  Philanthropist or artist; countless shapes
Of charity bless earth; but nought appears
Lovelier than woman, in her maiden years,
Walking abroad to misery's dreary haunt,
Soothing pale sickness, and relieving want.

The thoughts of her poor efforts spreading gladness,
  Filled her own breast with joy, that broke in gleams
From those large eyes, no longer dimm'd by sadness—
  A joy more light than young hope feels in dreams.
She looked a messenger of beauty born,
Sent on love's errand by the gracious morn,
Brushing the dew, as on her path she springs,
Goodness and virtue lending her their wings.

Across the dappled downs her fairy feet
  Shape their quick way; around her daisies bloom,
And seem to smile, her morning smile to greet :
  Beneath each step, crushed heath-flowers breathe
    perfume ;
The hermit redbreast, on the neighbouring spray,
Avoids her not, but pipes his cheerful lay ;
And the rough goat, as softly she trips by,
Looks in her face with mild, unfearing eye.

A rural village, bosom'd 'mid the hills,
  So primitive, so far from city-life—
Yet each poor dweller owns his share of ills,
  And that dead calm has oft its gusts of strife.
Here burn small jealousies, and passions dwell
In hearts that ne'er to high emotions swell ;
A little world, with all its hopes and fears,
Mirth with its laughter, sorrow with its tears.

And Sibyl entered the low cottage door,
    Where want, but noble honesty abode;
Her dainty foot trod pleased the sanded floor,
    Her grace on graceless things a charm bestowed.
The mother's face, where grief late spread its night,
Grew, as she saw that lady, quickly bright;
And ragged urchins crowded to her side,
By kindness welcomed, never checked by pride.

To give—what luxury to the virtuous soul!
    As the poor children kissed that maiden's dress,
And down the mother's cheek the tear-drop stole,
    In gratitude rough words might ne'er express;
She felt a joy as warm, as deep as they
Her gifts made happy on that summer day.
Oh, miser-souls, that ne'er an alm bestow,
How great your loss, what raptures ye forego!

Another cottage.   Seated in the sun,
    Bowed and infirm, an aged man is seen;
In life's turned glass the sands are almost run,
    He lives not in the " now," but what hath been.
Yon churchyard elms he planted, casting gloom
On many an early comrade's mouldered tomb.
Since he was young, how altered all appears,
Earth but the same, as slowly march the years!

Dimly he saw her.   Age, though cold, oppressed,
  To youth still clings, made glad by happy eyes.
The sun, in setting, seems to love us best,
  Lingering reluctant in the golden skies.
The ancient man looked long in Sibyl's face,
Won by her love, and cheered by youthful grace;
Thanked her for mercy's gifts, rose, forward crept,
Blest her, and blest again, till Sibyl wept.

One dwelling more—a shaded, inner room,
  A little pallet, roses on the sill;
Yet poverty, which deepened suffering's gloom,
  And sorrow seeming e'en the air to fill;
The mother moving with light, careful tread,
And watchful eyes, around the sick one's bed;
The whispered voice, the low, checked sigh of pain,
And the tired form, which sought repose in vain.

Such was the scene beheld by Sibyl there;
  Ten springs had scarcely kissed that dying child:
Sweet age, when every thing is dear and fair,
  The feelings warm, the bosom yielding, mild.
The pastor's daughter, striving grief to hide,
With loving smiles approached the pallet's side;
The stoic's iron heart might softened be;
Oh, when did death a lovelier victim see?

Slowly in that decline she pined away,
   Like a thin waning moon, with lessening light;
Her feeble limbs had shrunk, smiles lost their play,
   Her large blue eyes, with painful lustre, bright.
No longer streaming wanton from her head,
Her yellow ringlets o'er the pillow spread;
And the small hand, that once plucked daisies, now
Lay cold and white, as that poor pallid brow.

Sibyl breathed soothing words, and, as she spoke,
   Gave her the grape, to cool her parching lips.
Thus freshened, drooping sense again awoke,
   Though life would soon grow dark in sad eclipse.
'Twas touching, and yet beautiful, that sight,
Warm, blooming health—eyes full of kindly light,
Bending o'er dying childhood—flower begun
To fade away, ere opened to the sun.

The little one, her hand in Sibyl's laid,
   Gazed on that face where love and pity shone,
And both were silent; but amid the shade
   Which death on white-soul'd innocence had thrown,
A beauteous light now softened; 'twas the beam
From those large eyes, that seemed like gems to gleam.
Bright thoughts did fill the soul of that sick child,
And, looking upward, she serenely smiled.

All trusting, hoping one, for whom doubt's breath
    Had ne'er diffused its poison ! who shall say
But sinless childhood, in the arms of death,
    May see what loftier spirits ne'er survey?
Did she not mark some bright immortal there ?
Did she not talk with angels in the air ?
To spotless natures heaven is ever near,
Childhood to God, and watching seraphs dear.

She lay as in a trance, so hushed and still,
    So sweetly smiling with her loving eyes ;
She seemed some creature, in our world of ill,
    A moment lost, and seeking Paradise ;
A little wanderer on the plains of woe,
Too beautiful to linger here below ;
A dew-drop to unfolding morning given,
That only waits to be exhaled to heaven.

The dying maiden spoke in whispers low :
    " They'll place me in the churchyard cold and green ;
The weeds and grass will soon above me grow,
    And I shall feel no more—no more be seen :
Yet I should love the daisy there to peep—
Dear, humble flower—'twould soothe me as I sleep ;
And will you sometimes step aside to see
The mouldering grave, and kindly think of me ?"

But Sibyl, stooping nearer, kissed the child,
  And thinking she might meet her never more—
That soon death's hand would close the eyes that smiled,
  Her heart with stifled grief was brimming o'er:
She sobbed as for a sister, stroking there
Her arms, her shrunken neck, and flaxen hair;
And then she blest her, saying God would be
Her father, friend, through bright eternity.

Quitting the cottage, sadly weeping now,
  She gave the mother coins. Alas! no gold
Can bribe death's angel; all must meekly bow
  Beneath the dark wings that our lives enfold.
Childhood and age, the pauper and the king,
Must cross the valley's gloom, must feel the sting;
Deep trust in heaven, the hope of happier years,
Can only balm the soul, and chase our fears.

Sibyl the peaceful village left behind,
  Where joys may smile, but grief must also be.
She trod the path, by purple heath-flowers lined,
  Up the steep hill that looked across the sea;
The freshening winds, the glorious summer day,
The earth, the sky, betokening no decay;
The waves that swept with long-resounding roll,
Soothed her late sorrow, and revived her soul.

Bright Cornish scene, that mingled in one view
  The stern, the fair, the lovely, and the grand!
The mossy valley peeped the bald hills through,
  Like infancy, which holds by age's hand;
There beech and sycamore made greenest gloom,
And flowers, like brides their blushes, hid their bloom
Winds in that hollow lay as on their pillows,
And rushing rills set trembling yellow willows.

The old vaned church-tower, solemn as a saint,
  O'erlooked the dell; and, from its ivied side,
Burst the deep chime of bells, that, sweetly faint,
  Stole down the glen, and o'er the ocean died.
Whitening along the moor, where rivulets crept,
Boulders and ancient cairns in sunshine slept;
While far-off granite mountains reared their forms,
The home of desolation, rain, and storms.

The pastor's daughter, on her homeward way,
  Walked by the coast—a savage, wondrous shore;
The ribbed cliffs towered stupendous o'er the spray,
  While billows lashed their base with endless roar.
No foot might downward pass; but ofttimes there
The sea-gull's brood launched venturous on the air;
And when ships struck in storms, from peaks so high,
Ye scarcely heard the drowning seaman's cry.

She trod the narrow path, and frequent cast
　　A shuddering look where boiled the impetuous surge;
Yet all beyond was glory.　Ships, that pass'd,
　　Appear'd on floors of pearl their course to urge;
And white sails skimm'd the horizon's tranquil blue,
Like angels' far-off wings that heavenward flew.
Oh, God-created symbol was that sea,
Of passive power and veiled eternity!

Near crags that blackly towered, a lonely form
　　Now drew her gaze—'twas standing by the brink;
There bonfires had been lit on nights of storm;
　　Still, statue-like, he only seemed to think.
His eyes were fixed upon the waste of waves,
Broad rolling in, and thundering tow'rd the caves;
Then high he raised his hand, and on the air
Waved it, and beckoned slow, though nought was there.

Sibyl, unseen, pursued her thoughtful way;
　　He turned aside, and, falling on his knees,
Lifted strained eyes to heaven, as if to pray;
　　His hoary locks waved backwards in the breeze:
Some strong emotion shook him, past control—
Some inward pang or terror seized his soul;
And now aloft his trembling arms were tost,
And the low words were heard, "My soul is lost!"

The maiden gazed, and felt a harrowing thrill;
   She knew the mourner now. As some frail bird
The deadly cobra charms, so power and will
   Died in her shrinking soul; no limb she stirred.
One object fixed her sight—that sorrowing man;
Through all her veins quick, chilly tremors ran;
Her lip was mute, and, in that breathless hush,
She could nor move away, nor forward rush.

But he, so pierced by fear or keen remorse,
   Now bowed to other feelings. Speechless grief
Poured on him with subduing, softening force;
   Nature in such sad hour will bring relief.
Sibyl beheld his head droop low, more low,
And she could hear his long-drawn sobs of woe,
That told of thoughts where hope could take no part,
That seemed the wail of some fast-breaking heart.

The spell was loosed; the sight of bitter tears
   Drew Sibyl forward—a faint cry she gave,
Half of surprise, half anguish, blent with fears.
   She sprang, she reached him kneeling o'er the wave.
"Father!" embracing him, she wildly cried;
"Tell me your grief." He shook his head and sighed.
"Whate'er your secret be, your wrong, or ill,
I'll shield you, comfort you, and love you still."

SIBYL OF CORNWALL.

PART III.

TRELAWN was seated in the quiet room,
  Where oft his hours in mental toil were past;
Where classic studies charmed him, and no gloom,
  Till of late days, did retrospection cast.
It drew near midnight, and another there
Sat sternly silent, in an old oak chair.
A lamp before them feebly shed its rays,
And on the flame both fixed a thoughtful gaze.

With anxious sorrow drooped the pastor's brow;
  He once sweet peace and many a pleasure knew;
These, crush'd, o'erthrown, lay saddest ruins now,
  Grief and remorse the weeds that round them grew;
And yet his heart, obeying duty's call,
Warmed with kind thoughts, and cherished love for all
Whate'er his sufferings, still 'twas his to give
Joy unto others, and for others live.

The stranger had life's zenith reached, his frame
  Tall and commanding, black his ample beard,
His features coarse, his eye of dullest flame,
  Where no fine mind or genial light appeared;
But base self-love spake there, concentred, cold,
And there a tale unbridled passions told.
Though no true boldness on his front was seen,
His brow was stern, and fierceness marked his mien.

Silence was broken.   Lifting slow his eyes,
  Fiery yet sullen, Osborne proudly spoke;
The pastor's face betokened no surprise,
  Though every word was like a dagger's stroke:
" No more I plead; pride's iron shall be bent;
Sibyl I wed, so give thy full consent.
I love her deeply; every fear resign;
Thy life is safe, thy gentle daughter mine."

Trelawn smiled faintly—it was struggling scorn
  That curled his lip; but soon the smile had past,
And other feelings in his heart were born;
  The shaft had struck, the terror came at last.
Shall Sibyl's bliss be wrecked, himself to save
From bitter shame, an ignominious grave?
Or shall he boldly now the worst defy,
Bear shame, if shame must come, and dare to die?

" She loves, thou say'st, another," Osborne cried ;
  " Such early love is folly, light as frail ;
Sibyl will all forget it, when a bride ;
  My lands are broad ; birth—what does birth avail ?
I won my gold by slaves on Afric's coast ;
But gold is power ; I make no further boast.
Consent, I bid thee ; ask not love to wait ;
Aid me to bend her will, nor rush on fate."

A change came o'er the pastor ; sudden fire
  Flashed from his eyes, age burning vigour now ;
Yet anguish swayed his spirit more than ire ;
  He rose, put back the white hair from his brow ;
He clenched his hand, and, in the doubtful light,
His high-raised form still grew upon the sight :
" I do defy thee—let the tempest burst !
I will not sell my daughter—do thy worst !"

Osborne confronted him with careless air,
  His features wearing smiles ; nought recked his heart
How bled Trelawn's ; he only sought to bare
  Its wounds afresh, and deeper stir the dart.
" What ! art thou callous, then, to public shame ?
Wouldst thou not shield, at least for life, thy name ?
Will it be nought a felon's death to die,
The jest of mobs—the mark of infamy ?"

And Osborne watched him.   Firm awhile he stood,
  Nor heeded that keen, scrutinizing look;
But soon from flushing cheek ebbed back the blood,
  And his wan face a pained expression took.
He, the deemed godly man, who preached of heaven,
Thus to be branded, to the gallows given !
'Twas not he feared the tranquil, resting tomb;
But, oh, this horrible, this dreadful doom !

A moment for support he grasped the chair,
  And called on God to strengthen him that hour;
His soul half wandered in its deep despair,
  Though still resisting, braving Osborne's power.
Gradual he sank, and, while no word he said,
Drooped over trembling knees his hoary head.
Flesh struggled hard with mind; he could not shroud
That inward agony, but groaned aloud.

Osborne stood by, exulting, seeing well
  Nature had triumphed—that he clung to life.
A doom of shame—this, this seemed spirit's hell;
  Trelawn slow yielded in that mental strife.
" Consent, though she oppose me !" Osborne cried;
" And thou art safe ; no ill shall e'er betide;
I keep the secret."   Low the pastor bent,
And moaned in anguished accents, " I consent !"

SIBYL OF CORNWALL.

PART IV.

The noon was sunny; flowers breathed odours sweet—
   Odours of thankfulness for skies so fair;
The wren quick twittered in his green retreat,
   The fountain curved a rainbow in the air;
The spotted butterflies and tawny bees
Floated or frolicked, telling to the breeze
What joy was theirs, and fancying suns and flowers
Made only to delight their jocund hours.

Sibyl was walking mid the garden beds;
   Oh, tranquil and delicious scene around!
Red roses, with their hanging, lustrous heads,
   Sweet mignonette perfuming all the ground;
Scarlet geraniums, and the fuschia's bell,
In whose rich chambers fairies love to dwell;
Streaked hooded pinks, and pansies with soft dyes,
Catching their light and blueness from the skies.

Flowers, offspring of the teeming, generous earth—
    Flowers, the sole relics of our Eden lost—
So beautiful, so stainless in their birth,
    Something of heaven with dying nature crossed;
They breathe on outer sense ambrosial balm,
Soothe grief within, and bring the spirit calm;
Sorrow, mid cheerful flowers, earth's smiling store,
Looks up to Nature's God, and pines no more.

Thus Sibyl viewed her flowers with brightened eyes,
    Forgetting sadness in that bloomy scene;
Her cheek, from rose and pink, caught richer dyes,
    And in gay sunshine, gayer grew her mien.
With tripping step from plant to plant she passed,
And looks of pride on those most gorgeous cast;
But the small lowly flower she loved the best,
Kissed its sweet lips, and placed it in her breast.

Swung on its hinge the creaking garden-gate;
    A heavy step—a form beside her stood;
She knew him well—one who had roused her hate,
    But to her forehead sprang no mantling blood.
Calmly she greeted him.   In Osborne's mien
Something unwonted now, and strange, was seen.
He drew her to a bowery walk aside,
And to her anxious questions naught replied.

D

Sibyl stood waiting with down-glancing eyes ;
  Cautious he looked around, but none were near.
Then Osborne urged his suit. At first surprise
  Startled her heart, while thrilled a sense of fear.
His was not love by honest truth professed,
Such as doth echo find in woman's breast ;
But love where self was seen, all else in shade,
And rather it demanded, than it prayed.

Not yet Trelawn had forced his lips to say,
  His child must wed the man whom riches bless'd,
Though heart and soul revolted ;. terror lay
  A pressing weight on Sibyl's aching breast ;
But keen aversion veiled, as clouds will hide
The lightning's slumbering fire, she softly cried :
" I dare not listen—honour I obey ;
My poor hand hath been pledged since childhood's day."

Osborne was calm. Beneath his heavy brows
  A sidelong, stealthy, piercing glance he cast ;
He cared not what strong feelings he might rouse,
  If, awed or won, her spirit bowed at last.
He knew her in his power, whate'er befell ;
So the fierce tiger eyes the wild gazelle,
  Close held in griping paws : it cannot flee,
  And finds no pity in its agony.

" First love, they tell us, dearest Sibyl, claims
   No serious thought, its feeble fires will die;
As mind grows stronger, love lights other flames:
   First love, believe me, is a butterfly:
It sports an hour and perishes.   My soul
Bends now a slave beneath thy dear control;
Oh, wilt thou not child-feelings soar above,
Forget the past, and bless me with thy love?"

He seized her hand, and dropt upon his knee;
   Contempt and hatred only Sibyl felt.
First love to her was sacred; she would be
   True to her vows, if there earth's monarch knelt.
" Never!" she cried; " you wrong my woman's heart
It cannot act the changeling's worthless part."
And Sibyl from him turned, her head raised high,
Scorn on her brow, and anger in her eye.

No passion he betrayed, but, sternly cold,
   Before her stept, and firmly griped her arm.
A low short scream—he did not loose his hold,
   Bidding her stay, and banish all alarm.
He gazed with searching calm, yet fierceness too,
Till her eye drooped, her cheek lost all its hue.
He gazed, like one resolved to sweep away
Each barrier that opposed his desperate way.

" Sibyl, I love you.   Though my suit and me
    Your lips repel, I love you madly still.
No more a supplicant I bend to thee,
    For life and death hang now upon my will.
Thy early löve I ask thee to resign;
Thou must—thy father wills it—must be mine !
Urge me not dark-veiled secrets to declare,
A desperate thing hurt pride, and love's despair."

His words, like strange enigmas, Sibyl heard;
    Waves of conjecture seemed on waves to rise.
Oh, whence sprang Osborne's power ? strong wonder
     stirred
    Her bosom's depths, and glistened in her eyes.
" Answer me, Sibyl—moments press—be mine,
And wealth and calm security are thine;
Refuse with love's dear smiles my heart to bless,
And be thy father's self-willed murderess !"

She trembled—something dread his words implied;
    Though loathing him, she could not flee him now;
With asking eyes she crept unto his side,
    For more he knew than lips had dared avow.
" Plain be my words," he muttered, 'neath his breath
" Thine act will save him, or will doom to death.
I hold the secret; in my silence lies
His hope of safety; if I speak, he dies !

Sibyl, half paralysed, had sunk in thought,
　But now she started from her wondering dream ;
As if some hidden truth her soul had caught,
　Strong feeling lit her face with sudden gleam,
And indignation filled her—slander vile !
O foul untruth ! O schemer's wretched wile !
Accuse her father, if denied her hand?
Was e'er device more black by demon planned?

Sibyl, in deepest silence, backward drew ;
　Then, with firm-planted foot and head upraised,
A withering glance on that dark form she threw,
　And in her eyes her keen emotions blazed.
No more she looked the meek-soul'd, gentle maid,
Who, on kind missions, through the hamlet strayed,
Relieved pale want, with age had talked and smiled,
And soothed, with love and tears, the dying child.

But there she stood, a shadow on her brow,
　Her bosom heaving with unuttered scorn ;
A being, who to threats would never bow,
　Fierce as the tigress, by the hunters torn.
Hot through her veins an honest passion flowed,
And still with brighter fire her dark eyes glowed ;
Sweet weakness in her heart to strength had turned,
And all the indignant, outraged woman burned.

"Leave me!"   She pointed at the gate, her hand
  Trembling, in answer to the excited soul.
Her cheek flushed crimson, reason's strong command
  Unable anger's frenzy to control.
"Away! accuse my father? he whose mind
Is virtuous as an angel's, pure, and kind.
Depart this place—begone! thy schemes give o'er,
Thy presence shall pollute our home no more!"

He left, but only more resolved to crush
  Her towering spirit, and his ends obtain.
Oh, when alone, poor Sibyl, what a rush
  Of varied feeling poured on heart and brain!
Reason her seat could scarcely hold; a dream
Most hideous did the last brief moments seem;
But mid the emotions battling in her breast,
Sweet filial love still master'd all the rest.

Did he not hint some dark and dreadful deed?
  No, no, her father could not guilty be;
Yet strange his late demeanour.   She had need
  Of more than strength to stem that agony.
The godly parent and the loving child,
The heart that for her prayed, kind lips that smiled:
Would she believe it—plunge both souls in woe?
She whispered, sobbed, she wailed in anguish—no!

Sibyl against a tree, half fainting, leant;
   Scorn, which had flushed her brow, no longer shone.
Gone was the heroine's strength, and, as she bent,
   Her woman's bosom heaved with bitterer groan.
She called her father's name; she fixed her eyes,
With tears o'erflowing, on the silent skies;
And then they drooped and closed, and low she lay,
Nor wept, nor moaned, as life had past away.

SIBYL OF CORNWALL.

PART V.

SIBYL had sought her chamber.   There a child
  She hung upon her mother's knee, and said ·
Ofttimes her evening prayer; that mother mild,
  Dear guide and friend, now slumbered with the dead.
In moments of great trial, how we fly
Back to the light that once illumed love's sky;
Recall the memory of our infant wiles,
A mother's counsels, and a mother's smiles.

Long did she sit, and ponder on the past;
  "Would thou wert here, my mother!" Sibyl sighed.
Great, terrible the burden on her cast,
  Who would support her? who would be her guide?
Yet must she dare the task, and pierce the shade
Veiling the truth, more dread by darkness made,
Prove if the accuser had but urged a lie,
Or seal her fate, and life-long misery.

She bent her trembling knees in fervent prayer,
  Burying upon her hands her stooping face;
Her tears made wet her hanging, glossy hair—
  How sad she looked, yet full of touching grace!
She prayed that heaven, earth's gentle teacher gone,
Through sunshine and through gloom would guide
    her on;
And grant her power her trial to sustain,
And ne'er to sink, whate'er her load of pain.

And Sibyl rose with heart more calm, and smoothed
  Her tangled tresses and disordered dress;
As if some heavenly voice her spirit soothed,
  Her face regained its wonted placidness;
And quietly her father's room she sought,
Where the long hours he passed in studious thought;
And yet she trembled, treading soft the floor,
And paused and trembled as she reached the door.

There sat Trelawn, no book before him spread,
  Absently musing in his old oak chair,
With folded hands, and low-declining head,
  His brow less marked by age, than grief and care.
His child he saw not till his ashy cheek
Felt her sweet kiss; yet smiles refused to break
Across its wanness; but he fixed his eye
Steadfastly on her, without word or sigh.

And Sibyl, taking his cold, languid hand,
   Spoke of his studies in soft, anxious tone;
And then she stroked his hair, with all the bland
   And soothing ways, to woman only known.
She wished him to disclose his deep-locked grief,
Knowing revealment ever brings relief;
She wished to lead him from the thoughts that lay
Festering within, and wearing life away.

She knelt before him on the floor, and still
   Held both his trembling hands, and kissed them oft;
A tenderness her dark eyes seemed to fill,
   Her upraised features beamed expression soft.
" Oh, tell me why this sorrow, this dismay !
Think not your secret I would e'er betray;
Though weak, a shield before you I might throw;
Deadliest of foemen is a hidden foe."

Trelawn looked full into his daughter's face;
   " Then he hath spoken—dared to press his suit,
Building his power upon my soul's disgrace."
   His pale lip stammer'd, quivered, then was mute.
Sorrow and deepest gloom his heart oppress'd,
A heart that e'en hope's dream no longer bless'd.
Again he moaned, " A foe that seeks to tear
My child away, and sink me in despair."

" Oh, no ! I have defied him : " Sibyl said ;
" But tell me why his fearful, base control
O'er one like thee ; why pass thy days in dread ?
Crime cannot stain thy lofty, noble soul."
She rose in strong excitement, clasped his arm,
Pierced by sharp stings, and trembling in alarm ;
Looked in his eyes for answer, that suspense
Hushing her breath, absorbing every sense.

He could not speak, but gazed upon the ground,
And, as he pondered, slowly shrank away ;
And still she held him, for her hand was bound
By some strong spell which spirit must obey.
Piteous she called—she prayed him to declare
Osborne spoke falsely, threats they then might dare ;
Oh, what great wrong, what dire misfortune gave
His life to law, or made him Osborne's slave ?

Trelawn at length looked up ; with gathered brow,
And bolder eye, he seemed collecting power,
The nobler mind subduing body now ;
There was a hush at that sad, trying hour :
Shall he reveal the secret ? must his breast
Be bared to light, his crime, his guilt confessed ?
Yes ! his loved, faithful child shall know the worst,
Though shame may crush him, and his torn heart burst.

The pastor slowly paced the shaded room,
    And Sibyl watched his steps with anxious eye;
On his worn, aged cheek, intense the gloom,
    And at his heart intense the agony.
And now he stood, and spread his arms abroad;
His very misery Sibyl's spirit awed;
Then he moved backwards, as from some dread brink,
And, with pale face averted, seemed to shrink.

"He reels—he falls!" he whispered; "down, down,
        down,
    The boiling billows maddening far below!
One saw it; one was witness"—with a frown
    He paused and stamped—"our foe, our mortal foe!
But heaven forgive me—let me meekly bend;
To scourge my guilty soul, our God doth send
This evil, cruel man.   Now draw thee near,
And listen, if thou canst, the tale of fear."

Trelawn had ceased.   He looked like one relieved
    Of some great load; his bosom deeply sighed;
Yet his pale, trembling child, he half believed,
    Would start in horror from the homicide.
He sank into the chair, and hid his face,
O'erwhelmed and humbled by his deep disgrace;
Yes, humbling to a heart once undefiled,
Thus, as a felon, placed before his child.

"A murderer!" he whispered.   "Never more
  Wilt thou thy father love."   And Sibyl knelt,
Sobbing aloud, her drooped eyes brimming o'er;
  Yet tears but faintly told the pangs she felt.
"And I—I dare, in yonder holy pile,
To teach the way to heaven, though lost the while.
Dark, double sin, thus seeming good to be,
Does earth a culprit hold—a wretch like me?"

"Despond not, father, thus."   His knees she clasped;
  "Tho' man might punish, God will pardon all."
Her feelings choked the words she feebly gasped;
  He turned away, and stooped against the wall.
"My little one, my joy, my hope, my pride,
Will blush to own me, and forsake my side,
Will hate her father, and a stranger be,
And, when he dies, will brand his memory."

"Never!" she cried, and passionately rose,
  And cast her arms around him, while his cheek
Madly she kissed, and still, amidst her woes,
  Crept to his heart as if her own would break.
In that full burst of feeling Nature spoke,
Affection, like a pent-up torrent, broke;
Oh, can emotion purer burn above,
Than a devoted daughter's quenchless love?

" Never will I forsake you, did there cling
    All crimes unto your soul, all guilt, all shame;
Should love for you disgrace and ruin bring,
    Did all, who praised you once, revile your name;
Still I am by your side, to cheer, to roam
Where fate may lead, without a friend, a home;
Still I am by your side, while each has breath,
Your loving, changeless child, in life or death."

SIBYL OF CORNWALL.

PART VI.

Tired labour had lain down to wonted rest,
    Forgetting toil in sleep's restoring arms;
Cares vexed not with wild dreams the peasant's breast;
    No robbers, seeking gold, inspired alarms.
A rose-bud hanging on the parent spray,
The infant by its mother nestling lay;
The maid, from village tasks released awhile,
Dreamt of her love, her cheek one happy smile.

The flowers in every field were slumbering too,
    Sweet clover-heads low bending to the ground;
The daisy's snowy ruff was wet with dew,
    As, close in sleep, her little eye was bound;
The chaffinch trilled no more; the wide-spread sea
Just heaved and breathed in sleepy majesty;
And bright-rayed stars were gazing from the skies,
Watching the resting world, like angel-eyes.

Now only far ambition was awake,
　　Laying her plans for future power and fame;
And knowledge strove her quenchless thirst to slake,
　　In ancient tomes, beside the lamp's pale flame.
Now pain, from whose worn eyelids sleep had fled,
Breathed fruitless moans, and tossed upon his bed;
And sorrow, wan-cheeked vestal, sat apart,
Dropp'd the still tear, and fed on her own heart.

Among the last, the sisters of pale grief,
　　Sibyl was gazing on the placid night;
To her it brought no slumber, no relief,
　　Thought, busy thought, still putting sleep to flight.
Backward, for warmth, she flung the lattice-frame,
And cooling airs from heathy uplands came;
And, leaning on her hand, she wiled the hours,
Gazing on moon-lit lawn, and dreaming flowers.

All Nature in a breathless trance was lying,
　　From the green valley to the cairn-crowned hill;
She heard among the leaves the low winds sighing;
　　The faint, far sobbing of the infant rill;
Each wave that, at a distance, lapped the shore,
Monotonous, low-sounding, evermore,
On rolling, sweeping back, and resting never,
Breaking in snowy foam, for ever, ever.

And then she gazed upon the world-hung sky;
   Hushed all that spangled infinite of blue;
She thought if dwellers, in those globes on high,
   Passions like ours, and dread and misery knew;
Or if peace ceaseless blest those golden spheres,
Where crime no darkness caused, and woe no tears,
But God to man perpetual Edens gave,
Unfelt a sorrow, and unknown a grave.

The lovely scene entranced her musing breast,
   But could not chase the gloom that gathered there;
Nature looks ever happy when at rest,
   Yet oft, in calm, mind's rudest shocks we bear;
She felt more keenly, at that lonely hour,
Her father's danger, and base Osborne's power;
And loudly duty called 'mid heart's strong strife,
" Think not of joy! but save thy father's life!"

Instinctively her eyes now turned afar,
   Resting on ocean crisped, and silvered o'er
By the thin crescent moon; while many a star
   Shimmered upon its azure, glistening floor.
The scene woke thoughts of one beyond that deep,
Whose memory, faithful love, embalmed, would keep;
Whose name came back, like music of past years,
Through soul's dim cells, and filled her eyes with tears.

E

Plighted in childhood, round her heart had twined
    Affection's tendrils, till they grew so strong,
That clasping iron could not firmer bind ;
    Nor less did Sibyl love, for loving long.
And must she rend the bonds her heart wears yet,
Teach truth to lie, her bosom to forget?
O'er the sweet past oblivion's curtain throw,
And blight each hope, and quench each joy below?

Pain on all sides ; still Osborne's love to spurn
    Would give her father to a dreadful fate.
Should she accept him ?   Madly did she yearn
    To her first love, heart-pierced and desolate.
She moaned in unresolve, and whispered low,
The chamber floor her small foot beating slow.
Brave hearts the body's pangs will firmly bear,
But pangs of mind—O hard the conflict there !

The tranquil moonbeams, through the lattice stealing,
    Beheld at wonted prayer the pastor's child,
Beside the bed the fragile figure kneeling,
    The beauteous face uplifted, meek and mild ;
The pure light glossed her tresses, giving now
A heavenly lustre to her softened brow ;
Angels, while passing, might look in, and deem
They saw a sister in that lovely dream.

Prayer breathes sustaining calmness o'er the soul,
   In her most troubled moods; it is the bird,
True halcyon-bird of peace, when waters roll,
   And spirit to its lowest depths is stirred;
Support from God, the one great source of power,
Meek resignation in our trial hour,
Both shall be given to prayer, if breathed sincere,
Bright link between the skies, and mortals here.

Sibyl's low, heart-breathed sighs grew less and less,
   Till quietude fell on her like sweet balm;
No more her young limbs shook through mind's distress,
   But stole into her bosom holiest calm.
Now rising from her knees, she paced the room,
And by the lamp that softened gathering gloom,
She looked again the pale Madonna keeping
Her mournful watch, while other hearts were sleeping.

Then to her couch she crept, and laid her head
   In sweet composure on her snowy pillow,
An infant's mildness o'er her features spread,
   Her bosom gentle as a summer billow;
So thoughts from heaven can tranquillise, and bring
O'ershadowing beauty, like an angel's wing—
Thoughts flowing from a pure-waved fount of peace,
Bidding all inward strife and passion cease.

E 2

A sob at intervals—a murmur low
  From sweetest lips, like half-blown roses, stirred,
When o'er them evening's air is pulsing slow;
  Her head down-folded like a nestling bird;
To gentlest, balmiest sleep, she sinks away,
Insensibly as fades the dying day,
And on her face no mark of grief appears,
Save where her eyelids close, bright-fringed with tears.

Old was the smooth-floored room; around the walls
  Carved wainscot ran; the ceiling paintings graced—
Paintings that might have decked King Arthur's halls,
  Wrought in most quaint and antiquarian taste;
The windows, with their upright shafts of stone,
Projected far; the small round mirrors shone;
The place could boast nought richly gay or fair,
Antiquity's deep spell on all things there.

The westering sun lit up with golden sheen
  A narrow oriel of that ancient room.
Within it leant two figures: one was seen
  Stern in mid-age, and one in youth's sweet bloom.
The first all ardour looked, impetuous, bold,
Yet proud and threatening, formed in coarsest mould;
The last seemed humbled, though of spirit high,
And curbed by fear, though bravery orbed her eye.

Osborne to Sibyl's side had gently pressed;
    But she, with absent air and low-drooped head,
Concealed the deadly struggle in her breast,
    As all her former fear and hate had fled.
But now a last resolve her soul would take—
Move the deep springs of mercy, and awake
His better feelings, bid his honour glow,
If honour, feeling, heart like his might know.

She strove to speak, but paused with doubtful look;
    To fly such fate, what might not woman do?
With bursting, strange emotion, Sibyl shook,
    And at his feet her form abandoned threw.
Gone was all strength of mind; she trembled there,
Abject in woe, and crouching in despair;
Covering her face as if a culprit bowed,
While, woman's pride forgot, she sobbed aloud.

" Oh, pity me, if human be thy soul!
    If sorrows ever touched thee, pity now!
I envy those who feeling can control,
    And to the will of God submissive bow.
Yes, I may act a proud, rebellious part;
But wouldst thou take my hand without my heart?
Wed madly one who ne'er might give thee joy,
But, by repining, all thy bliss destroy?

" The truth I veil not; there is one who claims
    My faith, my vows, my undivided love,
From childhood's hour alike our dreams, our aims,
    Affection sealed below, to live above.
All fearful things, unfearing, I would dare,
But falsehood's blackening brand I shrink to bear;
Yet on another doom and death to bring—
Here my heart faints—here, here, the piercing sting !"

She raised her face imploringly; her sighs,
    Her struggling feelings, choked awhile her words;
Large one by one tears fell, and then her eyes
    A flood suffused; her thoughts were e'en as swords
Stabbing her bosom; rose before her view
Her father prisoned with a felon-crew;
She saw the gallows, heard the mob's wild cry,
The last to bear, more dreadful than to die !

" Hast thou a father ?   Oh, then feel for me !
    Dost thou e'er think of death, and that bright heaven
Which waits the generous soul ?   To thee, to thee,
    All my sad sighs, and all my prayers are given.
Have mercy on old age, so near the tomb !
Nor, for my poor refusal, seal his doom;
Pity a heart whose love from earliest years
Has known no change, nor quench its hope in tears."

She ceased, in wildest woe still kneeling there,
   Striving her bitter sobs to check in vain.
He stood above her with unsoftened air,
   And, on his heavy brow, no trace of pain.
One foot advanced, his hand was sternly raised,
And in his eye the will's fierce ardour blazed.
So lowers a threatening cloud at night's deep noon,
Sullenly rolled above the gentle moon.

Poor humbled one, whose acts had ever been
   Those of sweet mercy, and of generous worth,
A guardian-angel in the village seen.
   O virtue ! hast thou no reward on earth ?
'Twas sad that spectacle : the good, the fair,
Gazing on evil in her last despair;
Her fate all hanging on the tyrant's will,
His to make glad, or plunge in depths of ill.

He paused a moment, and his eyes were bent
   Moodily on the ground; his firm-clenched hand,
His lips compressed, all spoke resolve, and lent
   A sternness that enclasped him like a band—
A girding band of iron ; in his soul
There thrilled no chord to pity's soft control;
His nature was impassive ; self alone,
The moral despot, sat upon a throne.

Not loud his words; he spoke in accents cold,
   Measured, subdued, for feelings found not vent;
His cheek was flushed, his eyes, dilating, told
   A fiery purpose scorning to relent:
'Twas past—all words were vain; her filial love
Virtue might laud; a weak and stricken dove,
She might be struggling in the eagle's claws,
But nought to him high honour's generous laws.

" Hear my resolve—I set my soul on thee;
   Thou'lt love me better, when thou know'st me more;
Wisdom exclaims—snatch all the joys that be,
   For soon they fade on life's bleak, wintry shore:
Thy lot is linked—ay, must be linked with mine!
The bliss fate gives, my heart will not resign;
I can be gentle, dear one—soft as dew
On love's young flowers—I can be iron too.

" Then by the life I hold—by that dark hour
   When murder passed before thy father's eye!
By the round world we tread on—by the Power,
   If sovereign power there be, that rules on high—
I here make oath, unless thou cast aside
Thy first weak love, consent to be my bride,
Not forced, but seeming free in others' eyes,
The law its victim claims—thy father dies! "

Then silence a few moments hushed the room ;
   Osborne stood motionless, collected, stern ;
His eyes, fierce flashing 'neath a brow of gloom,
   Seemed with defiance, yet with love to burn :
Sibyl moved slowly from him ; all was o'er ;
Since prayers were vain, she'd utter prayers no more ;
Since tears would move him not, she ceased to weep,
In her sad breast her anguish buried deep.

Heaven grant her strength, resigning all which heart
   Had treasured up from childhood's happy hours !
With love's sweet dream for ever must she part,
   And mournful nightshade woo, for summer flowers.
To shield an aged father, Sibyl gave
Her life to bitterest woe—might duty crave
More from her breaking heart ?   A daughter's prayer,
Kind mercy, hear ! support her in despair !

No longer bowed by grief, or swayed by pride,
   A deep, unnatural quiet on her stole ;
Gently she moved her falling locks aside ;
   Oh, who might know what wrung her martyr soul ?
Crossing the sunset-beams, that seemed to play
Like heavenly smiles, herself as calm as they,
She walked to Osborne, spoke in mildest tone,
Then in his hand, unshrinking, placed her own.

SIBYL OF CORNWALL.

PART VII.

A SHIP at sea, no land to cheer the eye,
  Nothing but waves below and skies o'erhead;
Nothing to break that blue monotony,
  The round world seeming one vast ocean-bed;
The unfathomed deep now peaceful, now at strife,
Heaving for ever like a thing of life;
For ever rolling on, as at its birth,
Belting with solemn glory all the earth.

A ship at sea.   Oh, beautiful, when night
  Builds high her azure ceiling, silvery spheres
Flaming along it—lamps of virgin light,
  Hung there by God through everlasting years!
Ocean the floor of glass, where every beam
From those far lamps doth, softly mirrored, gleam;
The boundless space, uniting sea and sky,
Glory's grand home, the hall of Deity.

The night was calm, and every snowy sail
   Was stretched aloft, to catch the sleepy breeze;
Still as a phantom, through the moonbeams pale,
   The lofty ship went stealing o'er the seas;
The wave just curled from off the gliding bow,
A few small sparkles topped the billow's brow—
Bubbles that shone, then vanished from the eye,
Like moments melting in eternity.

The pennon idly wavered down the air,
   The nautilus her little sail extended;
Wide ocean strove heaven's breathless hush to share,
   On all, o'er all, the dove of peace descended.
As in white showers the slanting beams were cast,
The huge dark ship, rope, yard, and tapering mast,
Reflected, trembled on the burnished tide,
As if two barks went floating side by side.

The man on watch paced listless to and fro,
   Now gazing·upwards at the lazy sails,
Now counting the round stars, then whistling low—
   Thinking, as seamen dream, to wake the gales;
The helmsman grasped the wheel, oft looking forth
Beyond the ship, and steering for the north—
The dear-loved north; and, oh, that dearer isle,
Where fancy saw loved wife and children smile.

Glide on, thou bark! in peace and beauty glide,
   A little world ón that great, lonely deep!
The moon and planets watch thee; by thy side,
   Invisible, may guardian spirits sweep:
On ocean's vast, vast desert, One on high
Casts an unsleeping, all-beholding eye,
The far-spread calm, the softly-soothing light,
God's smile of love that stills the infinite.

But see, his flag of palest opal-red
   Day's herald waves; o'er all the sumptuous East
Gradually roses and rich violets spread;
   Voluptuous colour holdeth there a feast.
Not yet the sun springs up with flaming eye,
But from the horizon scarlet light-shafts fly,
Higher and brighter, heaven and sea in turn
Catching the blaze, till all things glow and burn.

He comes, and cloudless comes! flushed ocean's brim
   Reveals his forehead of hot, dazzling gold;
Round all the expanse of waters nought is dim;
   Like flakes of flame, lit wave on wave is rolled:
Billows turn rubies, as day's smile they meet,
Up leaps the dolphin warming beams to greet;
Light in rich streams thro' heaven's vast dome is poured,
And Nature, wide rejoicing, hails her lord.

The illumined vessel blithely ploughed her way,
    The breezes, charmed by morn, more freshly blowing;
White from her bow seethed back the cloven spray,
    With pearls behind, the fields of ocean sowing;
The sails her robes, all life along the sea,
Stooping she went, in grace and majesty;
Stooping she went, and walked the emerald water,
Glad as the waves, old Ocean's stately daughter.

Now upon deck the late dull sleepers came,
    In bustling crowds, to inhale the breath of morn;
Pale sickness felt new vigour nerve his frame,
    Drinking the breeze o'er freshening billows borne;
The maiden laughed, upon her cheek the spray,
Tripped to and fro, some ballad tuning gay;
The young child sported, and old age more high
Raised his bowed form, and glanced around the sky.

Fast through the groups the magic words were spread,
    " England is near!" They gazed across the foam.
Ploughing wide ocean, wearying months had fled;
    How yearned their bosoms now for much-loved home!
The sick man hoped to live, and sleep at last
Where their calm shade his native yew-trees cast;
For dread the thought to sink in this deep wave,
The storm his dirge, the coral-bed his grave.

The gleesome child was looking, with bright eyes,
    Tow'rd ocean's verge, for England's shore so dear ;
Her nurse had told her it was Paradise,
    Fairer than green ·Cabul, or sweet Cashmere ;
The stripling, long at sea, though still a boy,
Thought of his mother with deep, filial joy,
And loving sisters in their youthful years,
He, in the cottage-porch, had left in tears.

But one was leaning near the vessel's bow,
    With throbbing heart, more anxious e'en than they,
Oft peering through a glass, and from his brow
    Dashing the hair, impatient of delay ;
He chid the gale that bore the ship along,
Wishing its wings more sweeping and more strong ;
Bold was his eye, and sun-imbrowned his face,
Where hardship, toil, not years, had left their trace.

Mind breathed from each bronzed, manly lineament,
    Up from the heart light o'er his features stole,
And these proclaimed, in language eloquent,
    Beyond form's beauty, beauty of the soul.
Deep thought at times his gathered brow made sad,
For none who think are wholly light or glad ;
No stoic was he, feeling rarely slept,
But round his heart, in warmest current, swept.

And such was he who, since fond childhood's hour,
  Had dreamt of Sibyl—passion growing ever
As years lapsed on, until its warmth and power
  Seemed life's own flame, from which it could not sever.
Love knit the two; though oceans parted wide,
In thought they talked, in soul were side by side;
And neither doubted—flower in spring's sweet light,
Their love still opening, and with hues more bright.

Tresillian, now upon his homeward way,
  Resolved far Indian plains to tread no more;
Heir to a wealth undreamt of, he would say—
  Farewell the pomp of arms, the cannon's roar!
Henceforth the field of mind, for fields of war,
And learning's heaven-lit flame, for glory's star!
While love, which time will strengthen, not destroy,
Shall lap his trusting soul in dreams of joy.

Swift o'er the billows still the bark is dashing,
  Pointing to northern skies her gallant prow;
Eager she sweeps, the spray around her flashing,
  As though she knew her course near England now.
Tresillian's eye strains through the filmy foam,
He seems to hear sweet bells that welcome home;
He smiles, his lips in scarce-heard whispers part,
He clasps in fancy Sibyl to his heart.

Slowly the sea-bird o'er the surge careers,
  Betokening land—then screams around the ship;
And soon his glossy back the porpoise rears,
  Springing in play, again in waves to dip.
Great lord of life, the sun is brightly beaming,
Out on the wind the flag is gaily streaming;
Full swell the sails, all eyes are northward cast;
A cloud—a growing speck—'tis land at last!

Land! land! with pleasure glows the sick man's eye;
  His native breezes—yes, he yet may live.
The hard, rough seaman smiles; his cap on high
  The stripling throws, more force his " cheer" to give.
Land! land! the child doth up the bulwark creep,
To see her " Eden " smiling o'er the deep;
Then by her mother, mirthful fay, she stands,
And claps, with many a laugh, her tiny hands.

Speed, good ship, speed, and bear your living freight,
  Those yearning souls to varied homes they prize!
No one so cold, so lonely doomed by fate,
  But owns some friend where those grey cliffs arise;
And bosoms there, long mourning the departed,
Will soon again embrace them, joyous-hearted.
Glide, good ship, on! the very waves seem gay,
Flashing a welcome, sporting round your way.

SIBYL OF CORNWALL.

PART VIII.

Sibyl, in bitter musings, sat alone;
  Her pale, smooth forehead on her hand was leant;
Her form was motionless, as carved in stone,
  But on her cheek the colour came and went:
All spoke some fearful struggle in her breast;
Her eyes were fixed, her hueless lips compressed;
Amid her cloud-like hair no ringlet stirred;
Her foot was still, nor sigh, nor breath was heard.

Intensity of thought absorbed her mind,
  And held each sense; yet, in that silent trance,
That dream which could in-chains the spirit bind,
  Her very suffering beauty did enhance.
She likened one of those weird maids of old,
In Delphi's shrine, who fate's high secrets told;
Save that no frenzy lit her eye's full beam,
Her agony a truth, and not a dream.

Beside her lay a letter, but no tear
  The pent-up strength of struggling grief revealed;
From it she turned in silent, shuddering fear,
  As if some poison its white folds concealed.
It told her, India's toils and dangers o'er,
Tresillian trod again old England's shore,
And soon dear Cornwall's rugged hills would view,
And her beloved so long, and loved so true.

Oh, bitter task ! how meet Tresillian now ?
  Nothing he knew of her sad, altered fate;
Terror had made her silent ; must she bow
  To grovelling falsehood, feigning pride or hate ?
And yet divulge the truth—discover all ?
His reckless fury might dire vengeance call
On Osborne's head, and thus to every eye
Her father's crime in naked horror lie.

What ! through her act, shall that loved parent sink ?
  ' Never ! come basest falsehood, madness—never !
Let her descend—not him—o'er ruin's brink ;
  The die is cast, her fate is fixed for ever.
The dreadful tale Tresillian ne'er must know ;
But she, the falsest thing that breathes below,
Must front him now—the doting, loving still,
Turned to a scorpion, that can sting or kill.

" Have I not loved him since a trusting child—
    Love gaining strength with deepening, hallowing
        time ?
And am I forced to this ?"   With gesture wild,
    She raised her arms.   " Crime ! what to me is crime ?
I must be false, mean, all a lie, to save
My kind, dear father from dire shame, the grave ;
Must sink my soul ; I cannot upright be—
Cannot be true ; there, there, the agony !"

She hid her face and sobbed.   " And he will come
    With smiles, expecting smiles ; and I must seem
Cold, cold—my lips, that would speak rapture, dumb—
    The future blank, and all the past a dream ;
Would he had died ; for then I should but sigh,
Indulge my tears, and live in memory ;
Now he will brand me as the vile, the weak ;
Covered with blackness, while my heart will break."

And piteous Sibyl looked, with downbent face,
    Cowering, and shrinking from her own dark soul ;
But soon that weakness did her spirit chase,
    While calmness, masking anguish, on her stole
The duteous daughter rose, resolved, resigned,
Sinking all self, to youth's allurements blind ;
Prepared to drive, with ruthless hand, the dart,
And play the false one, blackening her own heart.

" Yes, let him come !"   She paced the silent room,
    A forced, sweet smile upon her quivering lips,
And on her cheek rich hues that flushed like bloom ;
    But, oh, that lovely eye—what sad eclipse !
" Yes, let him come !" still Sibyl whispered low,
With hands clenched tightly, walking to and fro—
" I will not weep ; I will not yield to fear,
But seem most cold, though fire is burning here."

Another sun flashed o'er the granite hill,
    And lit the bouldered waste where sprang no tree ;
Beams, too, made rosy many a limpid rill,
    Wandering, mid Nature's want, like charity.
The long, long moor was cheered by opening day,
The poor peat-cutter bless'd the warming ray ;
And early miners paused, to view unrolled
The huge round orb, through flake-like clouds of gold.

But chiefly Cornwall's vales rejoiced, a world
    Of happy life awakened by the beam ;
Alive with song each copsewood, dew-impearled
    A water-lyric hummed the reedy stream ;
The bead-eyed redbreast piped beside the stile,
And each small flower peered up with greeting smile;
The bee winged forth, and wound his merry horn,
And oak-groves rustled fresh in gladdening morn.

Brief time had passed, when, down the neighbouring
   steep,
  Tresillian, hurrying, reached his native dell;
Of each sweet scene a chart did memory keep—
  Thatched cot, brown orchard, and clear-bubbling well.
There had he urged the ball the greensward o'er,
Here led his tottering father, now no more;
And where broad patriarch elms cast sober shade, .
Had oft, when eve kissed earth, with Sibyl strayed.

Dear was the landscape as these memories dear;
  But on he passed, with quick and eager bound,
And soon, like one joy-wing'd, that house drew near
  Where dwelt the pastor, loved by all around;
Shrine, too, where bright eyes beamed, the guiding star
That lit love's heav'n, and lured him from afar.
Swift is thy course, O home-returning dove!
But swifter far will fly heart-yearning love.

The garden-gate he opened, trod the walk
  With palpitating heart: he saw the flowers
Her fair hand nursed; he saw the peacock stalk,
  And the tall clock which told the unresting hours;
The bees were humming as they hummed of old,
The fountain's fish leaped up with backs of gold—
All looked the same; yet something darkly lay
Chilling around; he could not now be gay.

No more, as wont, at morning's sunny hour,
  The pastor walked the slope, or mused sedate;
But there crouched low a house-dog, as may lower
  A sphinx in Egypt at a temple-gate.
Sullen he growled; but, at a word, upsprang
The ancient friend—the air with joy-barks rang:
He licked Tresillian's hands, he pawed his knee,
Bounded, and howled again, in boisterous glee.

Tresillian reached the hall.   A form drew near;
  But stillness reigned; the old domestic seemed
No more at ease: he trod with step of fear,
  And on his face no happy sunshine gleamed;
He mourned his mistress' sadness, wondering why,
Mid all things bright, tears dimm'd so oft her eye;
And thus he led Tresillian—one so well
He knew and loved, made silent by a spell.

They found her in the old oak room; her head
  Drooped o'er an open book, as though her mind
Deep pondered on the page; and, as she read,
  Her pensive, lovely face in shade reclined.
Tresillian's step awoke her; but her eyes
Betrayed no sudden joy, and no surprise;
Her face no flush suffused—all cold repose;
Slowly she shut the book, and calmly rose.

Oh, what meant this? not so he deemed his own,
   His long-loved would receive him: he had thought
Of sweet-voiced welcome, arms around him thrown,
   And kisses given, and tears with rapture fraught.
Forward he moved, his own arms fondly spread;
But Sibyl, faintly smiling, bent her head,
Her hand extending only, as a friend
Offers a hand, cold greeting there to end.

" How have I erred? what means this change?" he cried;
   " The cruel mystery, dearest love, explain!"
She did not speak, but trembling walked aside,
   Shunning his glance, as feared or giving pain.
Still did Tresillian eager questions ask—
For love like his a sad, a bitter task—
Urge her to give him answer, and declare
What his offence, nor drive him to despair.

Sibyl turned quickly with a softened look:
   " Offended me? no, no; but let me tell
The truth, plain truth"—her voice grew faint and shook,
   And on her brow the blue veins seemed to swell:
" What once we were, no longer can we be;
Friendship alone must warm my heart for thee;
Another claims me; youth's bright dream is o'er;
Whate'er in death, in life I'm thine no more!"

She hung her head, but, with an effort strong,
　Maintained composure, standing mutely there,
Like one to whom high power and pride belong,
　And cold as some white statue, and as fair;
Yet nothing hard, defiant, marked her face,
Where the heart's bursting love you could not trace,
But only saw her eyelids drooping low,
And a few tears that downward trickled slow.

Affianced to another!　Could the words
　Tresillian heard from gentle Sibyl come?
They pierced his trustful bosom like sharp swords;
　His soul was unbelief, his lips were dumb;
His loved, his fond, his vowed, from earliest years,
Sworn to be faithful 'mid their parting tears—
Could she renounce him thus—all falsehood seem?
Sure 'twas a fancy or some hideous dream.

"Tresillian, I am false—that word alone
　Must tell the tale; so hate me, spurn me now!
Hate me? ah, no"—she spoke in gasping tone:
　"Your hatred to the dust my soul would bow;
Spurn me, upbraid me; but, oh, do not hate!
Be still my friend, nor make more dark my fate;
Forgive me, and depart, and let me be
The base, frail, false—a dream of memory."

Her features sank in shadow as she turned,
　But he could see the rising of her breast,
Her cheek that now looked ashes, and now burned, -
　And the poor, quivering lips that could not rest.
Oh, mystery this! no longer cold or proud,
And yet her falsehood plainly she avowed;
He felt some evil secret hidden lay,
That warped her will, and dragged her soul astray.

He placed his hand upon her arm, and cried
　In no upbraiding tone, no anger now;
He bade her, swayed by honour, nothing hide;
　Was it for rank she broke her early vow?
Was it for wealth? or truly had she found
Another heart to which her own was bound?
Then would he ask not, beg not, hope not, more,
But brave his fate, love, joy, for ever o'er.

" Oh, cease this cruel torture! what is pride—
　What earth's poor splendour?　I am false to thee,
That my loved father "—Sibyl paused and sighed;
　She clasped her hands, but checked her agony.
" To save him—yes, from ruin, thou hast sold,
Sibyl, thy priceless hand for sordid gold;
But I am wealthy now, and gladly cast
All at his feet; believe his sorrows past."

Warm gratitude spoke softly in her eyes:
  " Dear, generous friend, no gold my father needs:
But I must cease; one path before me lies;
  Thus to be false, my once true bosom bleeds;
But false I am—must be—and never more
Feelings must know which ruled my heart before;
Thou wilt renounce me too, nor let love dwell
In that true, noble heart—dear friend, farewell!"

She gave her hand, her cheek's warm colour fled,
  She struggled with strong passion and blind grief;
No sob escaped her, yet you plainly read
  Wild anguish in her face, though flashing brief.
She stood again collected, moveless curls
Sweeping her shoulders, and her teeth's bright pearls
Shining between her lips that calmly parted;
Who would have deemed that maiden broken-hearted?

Tresillian Sibyl's hand an instant pressed,
  Then let it fall in silence: he had turned
To leave the room, his head upon his breast,
  But in his eye no harsh resentment burned;
His grief struck deeper than he dared avow,
For all unmanly outward sorrow now;
He breathed no parting word, nor once looked round,
Gazing, with hands close-folded, on the ground.

Alas, for woman! stoic she may seem,
  But when the bitter trial-hour is near,
She thaws like ice in feeling's fervid beam,
  Resolve's hard crystal softened to a tear.
Oh! will he leave her thus? his name she sighed:
"Stay—hear me—stay! and nought my lips shall hide!
Turn back—turn back—and let thy Sibyl be
All she once was, a moment, still to thee!"

Forward she sprang—he saw her drawing near;
  He opened wide his arms; with one loud sob
She sank upon his breast—that breast so dear,
  And their hearts, meeting, felt each other throb.
Whate'er the secret, Sibyl false or true,
Whate'er their griefs, one truth their spirits knew—
No spark had died of pure affection's flame,
Love's sun, in childhood burning, burned the same.

Oh, on them rushed the memories of past years,
  When in the hopeful present both were blest,
Ere they had dreamt of partings, wrongs or tears;
  A moment Sibyl in those arms would rest,
And he again looked down in her dear eyes,
Wiped her wet cheek, and whispered back her sighs,
His little playmate, sorrow once unknown,
His loving playmate, all again his own.

SIBYL OF CORNWALL.·

PART IX.

Sibyl would trust him, bind him by an oath
 Never to breathe the secret, for her heart
Could stem no more the torrent whelming both,
 Nor longer act the schooled deceiver's part;
Then would he see her strait with pitying eyes,
And call her falsehood duty's sacrifice,
Remit her vows, content that they should sever,
Parting with friendly feeling, though for ever.

And Sibyl listened, but no step was near;
 She drew Tresillian with quick hand aside,
Then tremblingly, with many a glance of fear,
 And pausing often, as she wept or sighed,
Disclosed the tale; and when the worst was past,
Her sad looks asked for pity, but he cast
His eyes in moody anger on the ground,
Rapt in stern thought, and lost to all around.

At length he spoke in low and measured tone :
  " I will not give it credence ; he, the mild,
The kind, the gentle—passions all unknown."
  Then fiercely did he turn, eyes flashing wild,
And, indignation burning, call down shame,
And many a curse on base-soul'd Osborne's name ;
Sibyl was pale with fear, and gently tried
To soothe his anger, clinging to his side.

But now they parted, one with stern resolve
  To search the truth of this too dreadful tale,
And the perplexing, fearful mystery solve,
  And tear from Osborne's craft the shrouding veil ;
One to lament the close of her first love,
Hopeless below, if hope might live above,
Duty the shaft which pierced her tender heart,
Yet holy in Heaven's eyes that ruthless dart.

The pastor in his study—would the hour
  E'er come again, when, with a tranquil mind,
Trelawn would nurse sweet fancies, and devour
  The banquet genius spreadeth, for mankind ?
When Greek would charm with beauty, Homer's song
Bear his rapt spirit classic seas along,
And hallowed lore waft solemn thought on high,
To muse on God, and bliss beyond the sky ?

Shall he again, with smiles of love and peace,
    Visit the villagers, his heart at rest ?
Now, when he bids their little discords cease,
    Fierce tumult shakes his own unhappy breast;
Now, when young maidens curtsey, parents bless,
Holding the infant for his kind caress,
. Though he may smile benignant as of yore,
Sharp anguish cuts him to the heart's deep core.

He sat in silence in his wonted chair,
    Gazing on some one nigh, whose soothing hand
Put gently from his brow the silvery hair,
    Then held his own with pressure fond and bland:
Tresillian watched him long, and, bending near,
Strove with kind words the pastor's heart to cheer;
The clouds, he cried, though black, would melt away,
And sunshine brighten yet his closing day.

The old man shook his head; no sun could beam
    Joy's light again for him; his fate must be
Closed in by clouds of darkness; one sad dream
    Must haunt him now, and in eternity.
His was a crime which man could ne'er forgive,
And yet, though great that crime, he fain would live,
By prayers and tears, in meek repentance given,
To atone his sin, and make his peace with heaven.

" And sad," he moaned, " to think that murdered form
Through me, through me, doth lack a Christian's
grave;
The body ne'er was found, in night and storm
Borne outward by the wild retiring wave."
" But hast thou firmest faith that Pender died?
That no one snatched him from the raging tide?"
" None—none! I dashed him over—through the air
He fell and shricked—he fell and perished there!"

While misery crushed Trelawn, deep-seated thought
Shadowed Tresillian's face: " I knew him well—
A lawless man, his heart with evil fraught;
Bitter upon your soul his insults fell;
And when his venom'd tongue did vilely pour
Slander on her you loved—on her no more—
I tell you 'twas not murder; lift your head,
Droop not in sorrow, banish every dread!"

" Yes, it was murder; no defence is mine;
I sent him to eternity, his soul
Blackened with many crimes.   Oh, Power divine!
Justly for me your withering thunders roll.
Why should I shun God's justice in this world?
I sometimes think 'twere best the shaft were hurled;
But then poor Nature pleads on terror's brink;
Disgrace, the gallows, death—I shrink, I shrink!"

He cowered and hid his face, as if to veil
  Some fearful image from the eyes of mind;
Oh, hideous double part!—he well might quail;
  He seemed God-fearing, to the poor man kind;
Still from the pulpit did he preach of heaven,
Still against crime his warning voice was given;
But if unmasked, how should his fate be borne?
How brave reproach, and bitter, mocking scorn?

" Say not one only saw the dreadful deed,
  That I might dare this witness, this mean foe;
If he accuse me, guilty I must plead;
  I will not stoop to falsehood—no, oh, no!
I would not lie before my God, to save
This hoary head from suffering, or the grave;
Osborne is silent now, but if his hate
Impels him to accuse, I yield to fate!"

He spoke his stern resolve in solemn tone;
  Virtue might laud that soul with purpose high,
Few nobler among Attic sages known,
  Choosing, ere trampling holy truth, to die.
Tresillian mused in silence; he could see
How strong, how deep, the waves of misery
Pressed 'round that hapless man, and felt one foe
Had power to save, or lay his victim low.

The pastor raised his eyes: " O God forgive
  My guilty soul, and choicest blessings pour
On this youth's head! in honour may he live!
  And grant him that deep peace I feel no more!"
Low on Tresillian's shoulder then he bowed,
And, manhood half forgetting, sobbed aloud;
'Twas sad to see those hopeless tears of age,
Repentance could not stay, nor love assuage.

SIBYL OF CORNWALL.

PART X.

Night fell; the barren moor wild winds were sweeping,
  The miner quickly trod his homeward way;
No star from out the hooded sky was peeping,
  No hermit glowworm lit its twinkling ray;
The valley's stream rushed darkly through the storm,
On the rough mountain bent the oak's strong form,
And thunders, booming, rolled through startled heaven,
Where every cloud a lightning-tongue was given.

The upper fire revealed the granite heights,
  Setting on cloudy peaks a ghastly crown,
Whose jewels were those fierce and fleeting lights,
  Ere in blue zigzag glory blazing down;
It played around the crags—a hellish game,
And lined the cascade's arch with lambent flame,
While on far shores swelled ocean's sullen dash,
More hoarsely deep between each thunder-crash.

The league-wide copse-wood clothing lower hills,
    Its wonted green turned blackness, sudden burns,
As lurid flame in sheets the horizon fills,
    And to unnatural splendour darkness turns;
Ever the skies pour torrents, that wild rain
The big, bright tears of Nature in her pain;
And ever the strong tempest moans, and moans,
Up the deep vales, like suffering spirits' groans.

Rage on, thou storm! ye torrid lightnings, gleam!
    Ye carry back the mind to those far days
When the round-world was forming, like a dream—
    Fearful, confused, all earth and heaven a-blaze:
When chaos strove, and thunders from the brow
Of rock-ribbed mountains pealed, as peal they now;
Such tempests tell the soul a God is near,
Who walks in calm, above this scene of fear.

But, look! as if that God, with sudden smile,
    Soothed Nature's pangs, and hushed her heart to rest,
The clouds that swelled in masses, pile on pile,
    Are breaking, and dissolving down the west;
Like wrath appeased, rolls off the thunder's roar,
The oaks upon the mountain rock no more;
And now, an azure opening in the sky
Looks like a slow unsealing, mighty eye.

It widens, and the stars are trembling through,
  Placid as holy thoughts, and silvery faint;
And see the moon, meek pilgrim, climbs the blue,
  Ringed with a glory, like a pensive saint:
The woods begin to sleep on crag and height,
Losing their gloom beneath that beauteous light;
The streamlet sounds like Nature's hopeful prayer,
And odour's soul steeps all the freshened air.

Such was the night which raged, then softly slept
  Along Cornubian wilds; that stillness fell
Breathlessly on a hill which, wave-like, swept,
  Green undulations, to a poplar'd dell;
There Osborne's mansion stood; rook-haunted trees
Clasped it in verdant arms, and night's weird breeze
Toyed with a myriad flowers—scene soft as fair,
But vice and meanness darkly harboured there.

Behind the house, along a tree-walled way,
  Two men paced slowly; their quick-flashing eyes
Regarded not the landscape, nor the ray
  The sweet moon shed while sailing bluest skies,
But burned with rage and hatred, and a cloud
Hung on each brow, yet neither voice was loud;
Each heart its struggling anger would restrain,
As we bind dangerous madness with a chain.

Osborne assumed an air of fierce command,
    And when he spoke, a scowl his features wore:
" I love Trelawn's fair daughter, and her hand
    I claim, defying all, so urge no more;
Wouldst thou the father doom and anguish spare,
Then silence keep, nor tempt the lion's lair;
Myself sole living witness, when we wed,
Trelawn is safe; we need not fear the dead."

" I seek to solve this mystery by a right;
    Sibyl, long since, by vows was made my own:"
Boiled Osborne's blood; the moonbeams, quivering
      white,
    Revealed a face where passion whiter shone;
He stamped in rage; he set his teeth—" Away!
Thou hast no claim; past vows are nought to-day;
Give to the winds young, puling love like thine,
Trelawn will perish, or his child be mine!"

There was a pause; how strong, alas! how strong
    The chain by which this man had bound his prey;
If lips revealed to others Sibyl's wrong,
    Hope for her father would be swept away;
Yet tamely, mutely, must Tresillian see
Osborne's mean craft, and cruel villany?
Gain no redress, and strike no vengeance-blow?
Thou God of justice! give him answer—no!

Aside Tresillian, with fierce gesture, drew,
  Then fronted him with stern, defiant air;
From eyes that glistened, steel-white sparkles flew;
  Like an embodied vengeance see him there!
Wrath from his path would sweep an evil soul,
Yet passion's steeds he curbed with strong control;
Words, low and slowly uttered, from him broke,
Hands clenched, each muscle quivering, as he spoke.

" Insult Trelawn no more, nor blaze thy shame;
  The quarrel now is mine; I do defy
Thee and thy malice, and dispute thy claim
  To Sibyl's hand—mine, before God on high!
The question hangs on thine, or my own life;
Now—ay, this hour, we front in mortal strife;
Bring thou thy friend—for me, I ask for none;
Honour my trust, and right my friend alone."

A change on Osborne came; his face grew pale,
  And tremors crept upon him, raised by fear;
Yet shrinking cowardice he strove to veil,
  By loud-mouthed mock'ry and facetious sneer:
He shunn'd the conflict; earth was far too sweet,
And life too prized, death wantonly to meet;
E'en if he conquered, what to him the gain?
No pleasure, glory, but unrest and pain.

Then rose the blood of him who, thus denied
  His burned-for vengeance, could not crush his foe;
And shall success crown demon craft and pride,
  And Osborne triumph, his own hopes laid low?
Thrice maddening thought, that such as he had power
To rend the parent stalk and gentle flower!
Thrice maddening, tempting thought—one blow might send
  send
This witness from the world, and danger end!

But Osborne turned to leave: " No more," he cried,
  " I grant thee interviews, and ne'er again.
I listen thy wild words; whate'er betide,
  Sibyl is mine, in spite of gods and men!
One aim I have—that aim I'll not forego,
Be it with pleasure linked, or fraught with woe;
Dwell thou in peace, and dare no more annoy—
Strange I was ruffled by a paltry boy."

The passions have their climax; the pent water,
  Though long restrained by dams, will burst away;
The hounds, long checked, that burn for sylvan slaughter,
  Will break the leash, and dash upon their prey.
The suns of Ind had warmed Tresillian's blood,
And hot it rushed, a headlong lava-flood;
His throat swelled large, wild rage his utterance stayed,
And rising veins, like cords, his brow displayed.

He bent an instant, clenching tight his hands,
   Advancing, stopping, glaring slowly round;
Then, as if loosed from reason's fettering bands,
   On Osborne rushed with one quick tiger-bound:
He seized him by the throat, and with a strength
Rage-giv'n, unnatural, held him at arms' length;
Osborne, half choked, could only curses gasp,
And sway, and stagger, in that iron grasp.

" Villain, to thy base purpose who wouldst bend
   An old man's sorrows, what may hinder now
But that thy spirit to God's bar I send?
   Death ends thy power; unworthy mercy thou!"
A pistol he drew forth; the moon's full beam
Quick on the levelled tube did play and gleam;
O dire temptation! rage, love, urged the deed;
One flash, the father—child—himself were freed !

The craven saw, and shook in every limb;
   Most dread, most horrible, to him the grave!
Trees, stars, before him swam, and all grew dim;
   But, "Mercy!" now he groaned; "will no one save?"
The wretch's terror, his great fear to die,
His locked, pale lips, his shivering agony,
Touched the more noble soul, in which was born
Pity's poor throb—poor pity mixed with scorn.

Tresillian loosed his grasp; he could not tread
  Murder's black path; he could not send to death
That man with all his sins upon his head;
  The caitiff turned, white-cheeked, with panting breath,
And he who scoffed at youth, despised, and dared,
Now all the coward's terrors basely shared,
And slunk abashed away; so night-shades fly
Before bold morning's honest opening eye.

Tresillian stood erect, with pointing hand—
  " Go, heartless, selfish, and most cruel man !
Honour unknown, thy schemes in meanness planned;
  Has earth seen baser soul since crime began ?
Go ! do thy worst—accuse, or silence keep !
E'en from thy love no pleasure wilt thou reap;
The scorpions of remorse will gnaw thy breast,
And on thy soul God's curse for ever rest ! "

SIBYL OF CORNWALL.

***

PART XI.

A LOVELY portrait decked an ancient room,
   Where oft Trelawn repaired to muse alone,
When evening made a sacred, mellow gloom,
   And sobered rays through purple windows shone;
A lovely woman's portrait, gentle-browed,
Her hair high-gathered in a sunny-cloud;
The look of pensiveness, the speaking eyes
Radiant with soul, and azure as the skies.

He stood before it in the amber light,
   Which trembled as it warmed the thoughtful face;
The dear-loved features drew his moistened sight,
   Beauteous as when she moved in living grace.
Oh, what a world of memories thronged his brain,
Waking past rapture, and delicious pain!
Kind art, that can restore the worshipp'd dead,
Gifting with seeming life, when life has fled!

Thought issued in low whispers, as his eyes :
    Dwelt on that portrait with unaltered love ;
" Blest spirit ! art thou now in yonder skies,
    Sphered in some star, all earthly things above ?
Or dost thou hover 'round me, here, e'en here,
Listening my words, beholding sorrow's tear ?
Wherever fled—oh, would that I could be
In peace, forgiven of God, with thee, with thee !

" Just heaven well knows that, maddened by his lie
    Slandering thy dust, I hurled him down to death ;
Yet shall I bear a haunting agony,
    A burden on my soul, till cease my breath.
A murd'rer—dreadful word ! I seem by night
To see his shade, and tremble at the sight ;
By day the cheerful sun is turned to gloom ;
Mine is God's curse—mine, Cain's pursuing doom !"

Shuddering he bent his head, and with his palm
    Shaded his brow, as some black brand were there ;
Yes, on his features, though so still and calm,
    The avenging angel seemed to write—despair.
Fain would Trelawn have prayed ; but might his groan,
A murd'rer's prayer, reach heaven's high, holy throne ?
Again he turned, and, with sad eyes upraised
Through softening tears, on that loved portrait gazed.

Long he remained to bitterest feelings given,
  Thinking if he had died years, years ago,
E'en when his treasured lost one passed to heaven,
  How much he had escaped of sin and woe!
Dreams, too, of love came echoing back to him,
And sweet gone hours, like some melodious hymn,
But soon, in memory's halls, the gentle strain
Changed to a low, deep wail of grief and pain.

Yet brooding thus upon his own sad doom,
  And nursing his own sorrows, he did yield
Worship to self; another, in life's bloom,
  Called thought away, and asked protection's shield.
Must he, to save himself, consign his child
To life-long ill, wrong, suffering on her piled?
Oh, recreant act! ye fears, ye struggles, fly!
He could but front disgrace—he could but die.

The pastor left the room as twilight fell,
  Shading the picture of the much-loved dead;
The tumult in his soul he strove to quell,
  And from his brow the heavy cloud had fled:
His thin pale face wore smiles his child to greet,
And she, with smiles, her father too would meet;
Each strove to hide from each, by falsest show,
Dear, kind hypocrisy, heart's bursting woe.

Sibyl was wreathing flowers, and softly singing
  One of the tunes of childhood, sweet and light,
And, like a bird's, her gladsome voice was ringing,
  When pipes that bird to sleepy day—good night!
Smiles on her lips that mocked at choking sighs,
A light from seeming joy illumed her eyes;
A glow o'erspread her face, while heaved her breast
With gentlest swell, as if her heart were blest.

She rose to meet her father, and his hand
  Took fondly in her own, with lengthened kiss;
She thanked him for his smiles in accents bland,
  Her own grief's night a morning now of bliss;
The struggle in her heart for ever o'er,
Calmly she bent to fate, would weep no more;
" Oh, 'tis no sacrifice !" she gaily cried;
" Thou wilt be safe, and I—a rich man's bride."

With searching glance he gazed into her face;
  Her joyous words, he felt, belied her heart;
There sorrow's shaft had found a rankling place,
  Gay words the feathers on the entering dart.
" My noble one, my good, unselfish child,
Thy cheek so lustrous, and thy look so mild,
I do mistrust; the bright cloud holdeth showers,
A snake is trailing underneath the flowers.

" Then know, dear Sibyl, thou shalt not for me
   Make dark the current of thy guileless life ;
Thou shalt not wed this Osborne ; well I see
   In thy young bosom, cruel, torturing strife.
Thy heart is all Tresillian's ; he shall shield
My blowing rose, and light and shelter yield ;
Tresillian shall defend thee ; to his love
I now consign my worried, gentle dove."

He smoothed her silky hair ; her sunny eyes
   Looked into his, with melting fondness beaming ;
A blinding rapture thrilled her ; in the skies
   Of her bright soul, glad thoughts an instant
     gleaming ;
Hope sang her song a moment to decoy,
Misery forgot, she only dreamt of joy ;
She trembled with strong pleasure, not with fears,
And kissed her father's hands, and shed sweet tears.

The old man strained her to his fervid breast,
   And bent in silence o'er her ; joyous dream,
In which, close-linked by fondness, both were blest—
   So blest, that neither did the happier seem
Oh, that truth's wintry blast should chill and blight
The beauteous Eden of their pure delight,
Scatter the flowers that love would nurse and keep,
Give age to tremble, and young eyes to weep !

Sibyl at length broke silence, drawing back,
   Pain on her late bright featnres casting shade;
It seemed as on an angel's radiant track
   A demon followed, and drear darkness made:
Doubt on her clouded brow, she slowly raised
Her asking eyes, and sadly on him gazed:
" How, father, can this be?. has rancour spent
Its cruel strength? does Osborne then relent?"

Trelawn had turned his face, and silence told
   The darker truth; unbowed was Osborne's will;
But now, with nerves more strung and front more bold,
   He seemed like 'one whose breast stern feelings fill:
With form erect and glistening eyes, he spoke,
Faltering no more the words that from him broke:
" Thou shalt not wed this man; come danger's hour,
I brave his vengeance, and I dare his power!"

Alarm flushed Sibyl's cheek, then left it white;
   Despite her mind's strong efforts, a faint cry
Sprang to her lips; she trembled in affright,
   Believing some great ill or danger nigh:
Osborne, his suit refused, she knew full well,
Would scorn all mercy, and the secret tell;
And must her dear-loved father find a grave,
When she, by suffering, might that father save?

" Oh, no, the fearful risk thou shalt not run ;
    No, Osborne's lips for ever must be sealed ;
God hath forgiven thee—what is done, is done ;
    Thy griefs to men shall never be revealed."
" And yet, what boots it, Sibyl?   A few years
I can but live, in sharp remorse and tears ;
Better at once to die my death of shame,
And thou be happy, and forget my name."

His arms beside him drooped, his head bent low,
    And his wan face the old expression wore
Of still and incommunicable woe,
    Remorse the canker at his heart's deep core ;
No feature moved, and humbled was his air,
You saw a man sin-laden, mourning there,
One whose earth-passions had to crime been given,
Though soul, with sorrow wrestling, turned to heaven.

Sibyl, in strong and passionate distress,
    Clung to his arms ; poor child, in her despair,
Half shrieking what mere words could not express ;
    Never the felon's irons should he wear !
Never, while power was hers to ward his doom,
Should law consign him to a dungeon's gloom !
His life, her own poor life she ranked above,
For that would barter hope, and bliss, and love.

She knelt to him, and gazed with begging tears,
   Then to his breast more closely did she creep—
" We'll save you, father, save you ! end my fears !
   Let us still hide the past, and silence keep ;
My duty done, and memories crushed and dead,
Happy my lot will be, to Osborne wed ;
Peace, safety, joy, will weave their lasting flowers,
And heaven's forgiveness bless your closing hours."

A choking in the throat—a few low sighs—
   A quivering of the lips, and nothing more—
She triumphed over anguish, and her eyes
   Flashed all the winning light they beamed before ;
She clasped her father's neck, and kissed his brow ;
He turned and paused, infirm of purpose now,
Argued again, with saddened, wavering mind,
Then, listening Sibyl's pleading, bent resigned.

SIBYL OF CORNWALL.

PART XII.

THE window was thrown open, and the breeze
  Pulsed softly through it—balmy, warm perfume;
The slumbrous rustle of the blossom'd trees,
  And songs of birds came gushing in that room;
Yet joy was not its dweller; summer laughed
On all without, and rapture's nectar quaffed;
Within, the tear down cheeks of sorrow stole—
Within, there gloomed a winter of the soul.

What unto her were flowers in vases shining?
  What lute or harp? their strings would only make
A mournful wail—the stricken heart's repining—
  And memory from its trance to torture wake:
Joy's outward beamings, when most fair, most bright,
Add only to the gloom of inward night;
And gayest sounds, in sorrow's listless ear,
Deepen the sigh, and bitterer make the tear.

Sibyl, her hand amidst her flowing hair,
   Sat motionless, and rapt in stillest thought;
Her little dog slept near her; none were there
   To mark the changes feeling in her wrought;
The light, the shade, that o'er her features past,
Like sun and cloud on mirroring waters cast;
The love that filled her eyes, then hate, then fear,—
The softness now, and now the look severe.

She mused on vanished days—the countless times
   She played with him around those beds of flowers,
Their voices sounding 'mid the old clock-chimes,
   A reckless rapture in those hopeful hours;
Her first affection must be now a dream,
A brightly-lapsed, but ne'er-returning stream,
A storm-rent flower, its bloom and beauty o'er,
A strain of music past, to charm no more.

But who can kill the memory? who command
   The soul to hush its griefs?   Alas! alas!
Love's yearnings are not furrows traced on sand,
   To vanish as Time's footsteps o'er them pass;
No, bosoms throb love's fire hath pierced so deep,
That, like the lightning-rings on some lone steep, .
Those lines of passion ever will remain,
One memory burnt into the heart and brain.

She deemed it duty to renounce her love,
   And pluck its roots, with hand that would not spare,
From out her heart; hard task it well might prove;
   Yet this, replete with suffering, she would dare.
Poor struggler in the net love's threads had made,
She hoped to free her soul, believed and prayed,
Thought herself strong, and toiled, and vigil kept,
But still was bound, and still a captive wept.

Sibyl gazed out into the sultry noon;
   The tardy clock now struck; the hour drew nigh,
When she was pledged to meet him, who so soon
   Would wander lands beneath a distant sky.
Though his impassioned prayer opposing long,
Her heart at length had yielded to a throng
Of mem'ries, and warm feelings; she would tell
All she had suffered, felt, then say—farewell!

Meet him?—the thought poured in upon her soul,
   At the same moment, pain yet speechless joy;
How shall her bosom its wild throbs control?
   And yet these raptures reason must destroy;
For she must bid him, in her heart of hearts,
A long, a last farewell;—and so departs
The summer-swallow, hope; but, winter o'er,
Her heart's poor vanished bird would come no more.

She trod the walk with step that made no sound,
  Lingered a moment by the beds of flowers,
Whose sweets revived her, gazing oft around,
  But no one wandered at those sultry hours :
Now swiftly down the myrtle path she went,
And reached a grot o'er which laburnums bent—
A place where bright-eyed mirth might revel keep,
Or moody sorrow count her woes and weep.

Tresillian, hurrying forth, by Sibyl stood,
  For long he had been waiting, watching there ;
How lovely looked she in that solitude,
  Though hueless was her cheek, and sad her air !
Here, gay of heart, they met in times long flown,
That hour a shadow on each soul was thrown ;
He gazed with loving eyes, but anguished brow—
His, his no more, another claimed her now !

Both, motionless and silent, stood apart,
  Their bosoms torn by passions undefined ;
The cord that long had knit them heart to heart,
  Did its sweet magic cease those hearts to bind ?
Did bitterness and misery swallow all
Tresillian's feelings ? dared poor Sibyl call
That old companion still her truthful friend ?
Or must this day e'en gentle friendship end ?

Her hands were drooping listless by her side,
  Her limbs were trembling, and her lips apart
Quivered but spoke not, while her eyes of pride
  O'erflowed with tears up-welling from the heart.
Yearning to one dear object, still she kept
At timid distance, though no feeling slept;
Ay, feelings warm as girlhood's fired her soul,
She only held their madness in control.

And Sibyl read his eyes all truth and love,
  As they had beamed in hopeful, happy days,
The lion-soul'd avenger now a dove,
  And momently more tender grew his gaze;
Yet was he checked by some strange, nameless feeling,
It was not fear, or pride, yet something stealing
Like sad respect his troubled spirit o'er,
Ne'er for his loved, dear playmate felt before.

Sibyl this change could honour, knowing now
  He reverenced duty's strong and sacred claim,
And more she loved him; but her plighted vow
  On her heart's sun, like sudden darkness, came,
And nature, 'mid that darkness, weaker grew;
Pausing and faltering, nearer still she drew;
But sorrow's flood its bounds no longer kept,
And, struggling all in vain, she sobbed and wept.

" Sibyl.! " the name in softest voice was spoken,
  Yet tremulous with feeling ; her large eyes
An answer flashed ; the chaining spell was broken ;
  Hushed in an instant were her bursting sighs ;
She stretched her arms—she rushed, and wildly flung
Herself upon that breast, to which she clung,
Madly as drowning seaman, on the wave,
E'er grasped the fragile spar that could not save.

And there she lay, her blue-veined forehead prest
  Down on his shoulder, uttering not a word,
Like a fond child upon its parent's breast,
  That sheltering place to all the world preferred.
O happy recklessness of sorrow past !
Abandonment whose pleasure, could it last,
Would be a bliss more full, complete, below,
Than the poor anxious heart can hope to know.

And he supported her ; too fleeting hour
  Of sweetness, yet of anguish !—from her brow
He put back gently the dishevelled shower
  Of glossy hair—his own lost, found one now !
E'en as the Orient bird doth fondly peer
Within the rose's heart, he gazed more near,
Gazed on those half-closed eyes, whose gentle light
Made all his day, their darkness all his night.

Tresillian silence kept; the stream of bliss
   That ne'er again must flood his bosom here,
E'en reason would not check; an hour like this,
   In its brief span, concentred many a year:
We live but in our feelings; lengthened life
Is not the dull, slow march of care and strife;
The youth who feels intensely, may expire
Older in spirit than the grey-haired sire.

But now he placed her on a rustic seat,
   And stood beside her with dejected mien;
Her loosened chesnut tresses swept her feet,
   As, whelmed by grief, more low she still would lean.
Poor stricken one! but midst her hopeless sighs,
A strong resolve now glistened in her eyes;
Her hands upon her breast were clasped in pain,
And troubled thought seemed busy in her brain.

She rose, decision in her lofty air,
   Dashing the tears of weakness all away,
Calming her mood, like one resolved to bear
   The heaviest load of ill that fate can lay;
And yet such fondness softened every look,
Her voice with such intense emotion shook,
She seemed, while strengthening, ruling heart and soul,
Revealing but more deeply love's control.

" I came to say farewell—to crave of thee
  Forgiveness of the past, and not to show
How hopeless and how sad my lot may be;
  The bitter stream, though strong, shall mutely flow;
O yes, I will endure, will brave my fate;
I do not ask thy love, and yet thy hate
Would bow me to the dust—the last, the last
Black drop of gall in misery's chalice cast.

" A gulf will lie between us; 'tis as deep
  And hopeless as the grave; it is as wide
As the broad waters of the ocean sweep;
  Truth, law, and heaven, will soon our lots divide:
Darkness falls round us; and to strive to see,
Regret, lament, were useless agony;
Then for my peace and thine, this meeting o'er,
Whate'er our fate, we meet on earth no more."

" 'Tis well," Tresillian cried; " yes, bury deep
  The memory of our childhood; think no more
Of solemn vows that linked us; keep, O keep
  Thy bosom by cold prudence frozen o'er!
At thy request to other lands I flee,
Naught my heart's wounds, my silent grief to thee;
Oh, would vain passion I could all resign,
And teach my spirit to forget like thine!"

Sibyl these bitter words acutely felt;
　Uttering a cry, she faltered to his side,
Clung to his arm, and e'en imploring knelt,
　Looked in his darkened face, and sobbed and sighed.
So beautiful, yet full of woe, she seemed
Like Mercy praying unto Wrath, while gleamed
Snatches of sunlight o'er her robe's soft fold,
And edged her floating hair with quivering gold.

Now, by a sudden impulse swayed, she threw
　Her arms around him, thinking to allay
His jealous, angry feelings; nought she knew
　That all his bitter dream had passed away;
His eyes flashed ardour, till they seemed to melt
In their own light of fondness, and he felt
His soul for her could yield each selfish joy,
Bear all, dare all things, ere her peace destroy.

" Dear Sibyl, I have wronged thy heart, forgive!
　In this wide world I know one law alone,
It is thy will; to do it I will live,
　Deeming as nought each feeling of my own.
For thee I'll joy to suffer, dare to die,
My greatest grief to cause thee tear or sigh;
If I might think thee happy, every pain
That pierces mind, shall launch its shaft in vain.

" Though it will seem as some avenger tore
    My heart from out my breast, to part from thee,
To hear thy voice, and meet thy face no more,
    The world a blank, and pleasure mockery ;
Yet, at thy bidding, self I will control,
And sunder from thee all save changeless soul,
Leave thee to God, my future path unknown,
And battle with my fate, my griefs, alone."

He sank his forehead on his pressing palms ;
    His bosom heaved, but murmured forth no sigh ;
Philosophy man's governed spirit calms,
    Stricken by sharpest ills beneath the sky,
Save the great sorrow of a loving heart,
Whose dreams are vain, whose treasured hopes depart ;
Thought, science, learning, all their proud array,
Still fail that heavy cloud to chase away.

Sibyl walked slowly from Tresillian's side,
    Pausing and turning oft with earnest gaze ;
She mourned to lose him, yet, cold reason cried,
    His presence would but sadden all her days ;
Approaching softly now, she laid her hand
Tremblingly on his arm, while sweetly-bland,
But mournful smiles her pallid face o'erspread,
For all her sparkling, happy smiles had fled.

And tears anon would trickle down her cheek,
  Like the large drops, that, one by one, will steal
O'er the moist rose's face when day-beams break—
  Tears wrung from spirit doomed too much to feel.
Never again that voice might greet her ear,
Never again those eyes, so fond and dear,
Beam on her loving light—the die was cast,
And she must smile, and gaze, and weep her last.

" Sibyl, the world may hold in lofty scorn
  The blinded slave of passion, and proclaim
Worthless the joys of love's sweet sorcery born,
  But love with me surpassed all wealth or fame.
Yet I would pain thee not by grief of mine,
The golden fruit unpluck'd I now resign;
The plants that sprang together fate must sever,
My dreams, through long years nursed, have fled for
      ever.

" Farewell! no bitterness shall taint my heart,
  I breathe no word upbraiding; thou hast borne
Thy share of pain and sorrow; now we part—
  Will our sad midnight ever know a morn?
Eternal Spirit, reigning in yon sky,
Heeding the lowliest when to Thee they cry!
Oh, hear my prayer, from joy's bright seats above,
For her I still would serve, but dare not love!"

He stretched his arms high o'er her, and upraised
  His eyes to heaven, invoking on her head
Each blessing mercy grants; and, as he gazed,
  All feelings, save affection, seemed as fled:
He prayed that heaven would pour its healing balm,
And time, the soother, bring her spirit calm;
Each guardian angel her dear steps attend,
Peace lap her soul, and God be still her friend.

Their hands lay in each other, and their eyes
  Were fixed upon each other; sorrow hushed
Each voice to whispers, and low, broken sighs,
  As on their hearts warm tides of feeling rushed:
Their language was no longer of the tongue,
But looks and gestures, and they madly wrung
Joy e'en from suffering, like intensest light
Flashed from the thunder-cloud 'mid stormy night.

And there they lingered, knowing they must part,
  Yet loth that hour to tear themselves away—
Magnetic influence linking heart to heart,
  While striving duty's mandate to obey:
The fond companions of a joyous youth,
Still in their thoughts, their souls, all warmth and truth,
Victims of wrong, their love but crime and pain,
And asking for hope's balm, in vain—in vain.

Grief choked their murmured words ; they felt how hard
   For those who truly love, to say farewell !
Yet must they breathe it, and their souls be barred
   From all they prized ; that word was as a knell
Of happy days to bless their hearts no more,
And dreams of wedded joy for ever o'er :
Alas ! for love, when all its roses die,
And the sad cypress claims the tear and sigh !

Once more her hand was trembling in his own,
   Once more to quit the spot her foot essayed ;
Once more a burst of grief, a smothered groan,
   Quivering of lips that faintly blest and prayed ;
Then, firm-resolving, Sibyl broke at last
From him who held, and through the foliage pass'd ;
Tresillian watched her, scarcely drawing breath,
Feeling his heart had given her unto death.

SIBYL OF CORNWALL.

PART XIII.

Up from the Eastern desert, still as fair,
  Like a broad glossy lotus, springs the moon;
Slowly she climbs the blue, no wandering air
  Ruffling the palm in night's hushed, solemn noon.
Sweet pilgrim, travelling through a hundred ages,
Gilding the tombs of priests, and kings, and sages,
She walks as freshly young, and meekly bright,
As when the Pharaohs blest her placid light.

But they are dust, in yon tomb-caverns hid,
  And dim oblivion wraps each royal name;
Slow crumbles each stupendous pyramid,
  Less fleeting only than poor human fame.
Rock-shrines, though mighty, fall and pass away,
Time on man's noblest works will write decay,
God's only are eternal; so the brow
Of yon fair moon in heav'n is brilliant now.

See where on sleeping Nile her beam she flings,
    Making a mirror of each quivering wave,
Crowning with glory the dark tombs of kings!
    So would she smile were all our world a grave.
The ob'lisk casts long shadows to the west,
In robes of light each hoary sphinx is drest,
Till each unearthly giant creature seems
Starting to life midst showers of silvery beams.

The desert-flower a moment opes her eye,
    Wondering how glows such splendour in the night;
The graceful palm stands carved against the sky,
    Its outer drooping foliage laced with light:
Stoled Desolation, with calm, folded hands,
Amidst a forest of bald pillars stands,
Softens her horror 'neath that heavenly ray,
And mocks less grimly glory past away.

'Tis now hoar Thebes unto the gazer seems
    A city of enchantment; silent death
Walks the grey ruins, while aërial dreams
    People the shrines, and give stone-statues breath.
Oh, what are living cities with their strife,
Their blind and plodding crowds, their burning life,
To grand dead cities—tombs of years gone by,
Awing the soul, awaking memory's sigh?

Where are ye, perished millions, in old day
   Crowding this now deserted, voiceless shore?
Are ye but mummies in yon caverns grey,
   Your friends the bats and darkness evermore?
Say, do your shadows haunt these ruins still,
Sigh by the Nile, and skim the desert hill;
Or in the deep, dark realms of Hades dwell,
Bidding to earth and sky a long farewell?

O mystery unresolved by reason's power!
   Man, sport of fate, the seeming heir of woe!
He weeps and laughs, toils, dreams his little hour,
   Then joins the myriads in the unknown below:
The universe still is—the stars, the sky,
And rests on all things God's unsleeping eye;
The visible hath been, and still must be,
Fair, glorious, or sublime,—but what are we?

Spirits who dare look up from earth to heaven,
   And feel we are a portion of that whole
Dowered with unending life, to whom is given
   Power over time, whose shaft ne'er strikes the soul;
Spirits that, floating here, or raised above,
Glow with aspiring thought, and thrill with love—
Spirits, the breath of Him who cannot die,
Living earth's hour to grasp eternity.

I

In Karnac's vast and solitary hall,
  He leant against a pillar lotus-crowned ;
Vainly for him past ages spread their pall ;
  Vainly the virgin moonbeams shimmered round,
Clothing the mighty ruin with a glory,
Whose every fragment told a by-gone story ;
Nor did he hear the owl that sat on high,
In Pharaoh's palace, hooting to the sky.

Oh, fruitless dream of dreams, the hope to flee
  From haunting thought, and memory's sleepless spell !
To change our place is not, alas ! to be
  Changed in the soul—this makes our heaven or hell.
To fly from love, the vainest dream of all ;
Passion in solitude confirms its thrall ;
In busy scenes, if burned love's mystic fire,
Mid Karnac's ruins shall its torch expire ?

Say, why have poets crowned young love with flowers,
  Wreathed him with smiles, and filled his eyes with
    light ?
Too often he brings tears in blood-like showers,
  And folds the spirit in a starless night.
Giver of joy unspeakable art thou,
O love, when answered smiles illume thy brow ;
A god of evil thou canst also be,
Shafts tipped with poison ofttimes hurled by thee.

He left wild Cornwall's hills—the haunts of old
  Dear-treasured memories love would guard and keep,
To traverse burning deserts, and to hold
  Communion with the ruin, and to sweep
In thought across the sea of vanished years,
To muse on races dead, on saints and seers,
Who kindled fires on time's most distant shore,
Mind-flashing beacons to go out no more.

And doth he hope to banish the one dream?
  The one great sorrow from his soul to sever?
Shall Egypt's darkness all blot out the beam
  Of Sibyl's beauty, love forgot for ever?
Will the good pastor's image cease to rise?
Shall he not hear those self-upbraiding sighs,
Mourning the act which laid his fellow low—
The cause of all their ill, and all their woe?

Oppressed and sad, yet nursing lofty thought,
  Tresillian paced from pillared hall to hall;
The midnight wind the hyena's howlings brought,
  Strange figures stared from crumbling shaft and wall,
And hieroglyphs perplexed him as he passed;
Mystery and terror on the scene were cast;
Time had cut down man's pomp with scythe of flame,
A ghostly voice from long-tombed ages came.

He sat beside the Nile ; an ancient palm,
  Between him and the moon, its broad leaves spread ;
It stood like death amidst the breezeless calm,
  Or sorrow mourning busy Nations fled.
His boat was floating idly on the river,
Whose wavelets crept and curled with silvery quiver ;
His Arab guide lay hushed, in slumber bound,
' Reckless of Thebes, and all the glories round.

Hark ! what arrests the musing pilgrim's ear ?
  From yon acacia thickets by the stream,
Suddenly breaks a warbling rich and clear ;
  Like music heard in some ecstatic dream ;
The breast of silence gave that music birth,
As poured by viewless fairies from the earth,
For nothing met the eye, while that full sound
Swelled o'er the wave, and steeped the air around.

The ruins heard it—the sad, mouldering shrine,
  The melancholy halls, the sweet notes filled ;
They flowed, as floweth soul-reviving wine,
  And Desolation's heart with pleasure thrilled.
A cloud obscured the moon, then ceased the lay,
Dying, with failing light, in trills away ;
Ye only heard low winds thro' pillars sigh,
And Nile's small waves faint-sobbing, gurgling by.

Again the moon in stainless azure sailed,
    Again burst forth the rich Elysian song,
As if some wandering seraph Nature hailed,
    Dropping down music as he passed along.
The notes were quick, now high, now warbled low,
Intensest feeling in their mellow flow;
They gushed in joy, and then appeared to borrow
Half their soft dying spell from hidden sorrow.

Sweet nightingale! thou lone love-stricken bird!
    What dost thou in this dreary seat of tombs?
Thy ravishing, sky-music should be heard
    Where fancy dwells, and Nature's beauty blooms.
Hast thou, from Delta's gardens southward winging,
Lost thy wild way, so wholly rapt in singing?
Like some good heart that wanders into crime,
Leaving behind it Heaven's immortal clime.

Tresillian listened to that magic lay,
    Fluting, and murmuring with the murmuring Nile,
And as he drank the sounds, more bright the ray
    Flashed in his eye, his features wore a smile.
Slowly he bent his head in musings sweet,
His gathered brow his tremulous fingers beat;
How slight a thing may rouse a lengthened train
Of thoughts and dreams long dormant in the brain!

That plaintive music fond remembrance woke
　　Of other warblings of a dearer bird,
The tuneful thrush that oft Eve's silence broke,
　　The piping thrush in Cornwall's valleys heard.
He leant amid the ruins, but his mind
Was far away, to early dreams resigned;
Scenes loved in boyhood round him rose, and threw
On memory's world warm rapture's rosy hue.

He seemed to walk the shore at twilight hour,
　　Long years ago; 'twas Summer, and the song
Of thrush and white-throat from the hawthorn bower,
　　Swelled like a cloud of incense, rich and strong;
He drank the sounds that floated far and wide,
Another too was listening at his side;
And both were young, and never cause for tears
Had shadowed yet their happy, golden years.

They searched for shells and pebbles, Sibyl's hand
　　Playfully trailing sea-weed, while most sweet
Her silvery laughter rang, and, on the sand,
　　Still nimbly flew her fairy, twinkling feet;
And now they stopped, and listened once again
That loved bird-music floating down the glen,
Which made the wide air pulse with life, and stole
With sympathetic influence o'er each soul.

They stood together, drawing nearer, till
    Their faces met—their happy faces met ;
The curls that touched his cheek would send a thrill
    To his boy heart—that heart would ne'er forget.
Love's meaning scarce he knew, but 'twas a joy
Thus to be near her, and that maiden coy
Would smile and blush in innocent surprise,
To read such ardour in her playmate's eyes.

And thus they wandered 'mid the failing light,
    Each to the other dear, they asked not why ;
Eve's bird, far peasants' voices, coming night,
    The green of earth, the glory of the sky,
Softened their jocund spirits, and, more grave,
They viewed the shaded hills, and purpled wave,
And neither spoke, while walking slow apart,
Sibyl with downcast eyes and beating heart.

Oh, first and guileless love ! oh, happy dream !
    To muse upon it now did yield a bliss,
Yet a deep grief—sick memory's saddest theme ;
    'Twas to his spirit like a dark abyss
Of sorrow with no bottom ; ay, to think
On that dear past, was rapture on the brink
Of some dread precipice ; below, below,
There lay the danger, there the rocks of woe !

Then full of freshness, with a heart of truth,
   She smiled upon him, bright with hope and glee,
Unsoiled in wing the butterfly of youth,
   Joy's bark all gay on summer's bounding sea :
Their sports the same, each mind the same had grown,
The lovely world seemed made for them alone ;
As misers treasure gold, he held her dear,
And felt as nothing could divide them here.

Now—bitter mockery of that blissful past,
   All, all had changed; the love of youthful hour,
With its warm light, was into shadow cast;
   Another plucked his early cherished flower ;
She who, sweet blossom, should have found her rest,
Sheltered from life's rude tempest, on his breast,
Must now renounce his love, and hide her tears,
While he must wander through the hopeless years.

SIBYL OF CORNWALL.

PART XIV.

Away! the desert lies before him; there
  The everlasting wilderness of sand
Seems, like his spirit, desolate and bare;
  And Civilisation, with her plastic hand,
Hath never city reared to coop mankind,
Or freedom's glorious arm with fetters bind,
Bid the foul poison-streams of lux'ry flow,
Or, by increasing wants, to heighten woe.

But man exists as God at first ordained,
  No crouching worship to his fellow given;
The ground he treads no grasping lord hath gained,
  He owns no master save the One in heaven.
The palm, the rocks, the wild goat, and the well,
These are his riches, pleased 'mid these to dwell;
Science he asks not, knowledge brings not joy,
For lofty dreams will sweet content destroy.

Tresillian scoured the desert on his steed,
  Sat 'neath the date-tree, heard the fountain's flow,
To parched and weary pilgrims in their need,
  Like paradisal nectar dropped below.
He strove to wean his thoughts from that far world,
Where proud advancement hath her flag unfurled,
Learn with earth's primal sons to dread no morrow,
To mourn no past, forgetting care and sorrow.

'Twas eve; the sun was drowsing in the west,
  Transmuting quivering sands to molten gold;
The antelope and ostrich sought their rest,
  Hushed Nature penned the desert as a fold,
When, with his guide, Tresillian reached a well;
Soft tinkled many a camel's silvery bell;
There friendly Arabs passed the tranquil hour,
Lured by the crystal wave, green herb and flower.

The scene was pleasing, breathing thoughtful calm;
  Their water-skins the Arab maidens filled;
The elders sat in groups beneath the palm,
  And one the Koran read, in letters skilled:
Some smoked, some strolled apart, and on the sand
Sported a swarthy, little black-eyed band—
Children still happy, be their home below
The scorching line, or girt by polar snow.

Tresillian by his bounty won good will,
  And mingled with those wanderers of the waste;
Their pledge once giv'n, they would nor rob, nor kill,
  The Frank was safe as in a castle placed.
He talked and smiled, but suddenly his eye
Fell on an Arab moving stealthy by;
Though robe and turban gave him Eastern grace,
No Oriental's seemed that moody face.

" Art thou a Frank?" Tresillian breathless said;
  Surely those sun-bronzed features once he knew;
Oh, idle dream—the Arab turned his head,
  And now they fronted, and still nearer drew:
Both gazed and gazed; Tresillian backward bent,
As much in awe as mute astonishment;
Was it his wraith—the unbodied spirit fled?
Had the deep sea sent forth the long-since dead?

The setting sun lit full the stranger's face;
  'Twas he! 'twas he!—they knew each other now;
Emotion ceased in one; ye could but trace
  A reckless daring on his sullen brow;
·But strange, and terrible, Tresillian's look,
His cheek was blanched, each limb, as palsied, shook
And still he gazed with widening, staring eye,
His white lips uttering but a feeble cry.

Unconsciously the man's strong arm he grasped,
  And held him like a vice; a broken stream
Of words that choking came, at length he gasped:
  " He lives! he lives! it is no mocking dream !"
Then trembling, yielding, he relaxed his hand,
Bowed slowly down, and sank upon the sand,
And, muttering fainter words, together prest
His lifted palms—" Found! found! my God be blest !"

In wonder they grouped 'round him; it was long
  Ere he shaped language calmly to explain
Why feelings overpowered him all so strong;
  Then to one ear he spoke, nor spoke in vain:
The rustic, men deemed dead, was tracked at last,
Was living here—oh, long-nursed horror past !
Whate'er the myst'ry, virtue, lift thy brow—
No felon was Trelawn—no murderer now !

Tresillian, curbing fiery haste, besought
  The exiled peasant his strange tale to tell;
Pender the truth unfolded, veiling nought;
  When down the cliff to seeming death he fell,
And Osborne, the " sole witness," standing near,
Beheld him topple o'er those rocks of fear,
Dashed by incensed Trelawn, whose feeble age
Had won unnatural strength from burning rage:

He did not perish, though none recked his call,
  He did not sink in the tempestuous wave—
A jutting tree had stayed his headlong fall,
  And Pender, clinging there, escaped a grave.
That night in secret, stained himself with crime,
He joined a crew, and sailed for foreign clime;
He cared not if men deemed him with the dead,
He only loathed his land, and, loathing, fled.

Yet 'twas not hate alone which kept him there—
  Osborne had learnt he wandered, living still:
" Knew Osborne this ?" Tresillian cried, a glare
  Flashing in eyes that fury seemed to fill:
Osborne with gold had bribed him still to roam,
That gold to cease if e'er he ventured home;
Thus Moslem he had turned, and hid him here,
Loving these wastes, the wanderer's wild career.

" Thou Osborne, lying, mean, perfidious knave,
  More subtile than the adder, black than hell !"
So inly spoke Tresillian, who would brave
  Passion's sharp goadings, and his feelings quell;
But now from dread and shame Trelawn to free,
And rescue Sibyl—task of ecstasy !
Oh, doth she mourn, and still ward off her fate ?
Or may they homeward fly—too late, too late ?

Gold should be Pender's passing all his dreams,
  Would he to England's shores return that hour;
The peasant, duped no more by Osborne's schemes,
  Happy would go, would crush this caitiff's power;
The compact sealed on that far desert sand,
God they invoked, and shook each other's hand;
Oh, still may Sibyl struggle with her fate,
Or shall they homeward fly—too late, too late?

SIBYL OF CORNWALL.

PART XV.

THE moon was sailing, like a Northern bark,
   Among the drifting icebergs of the clouds,
Now veiled, now sprinkling silver on the dark ;
   The stars o'er-arched the hills in golden crowds ;
The broad, bleak moor stretched on without a tree,
Savage and lone in Nature's poverty,
Grey cairn and funeral barrow there uppiled,
Bald Desolation king of all that wild.

Two steeds along the flinty road were dashing,
   Their flanks all white with foam, their nostrils spread,
And from their clattering hoofs quick sparks were flashing;
   It seemed for life or death the horsemen sped.
The younger ofttimes viewed the Eastern skies,
As though he feared the day too soon would rise,
Then spurred once more his headlong, generous steed,
And urged his comrade to redoubled speed.

Tresillian reached last eve the longed-for shore,
   And friendly lips had told him of the day
When Sibyl would be wedded ; that night o'er,
   A martyr bride, she would her lord obey.
Yes, oft amid the changeful scenes of life,
We reach a point with joy or misery rife,
Just at the eventful time ; Tresillian came,
And the sad tidings filled his breast with flame.

Still plunged the horsemen o'er the boulder'd waste ;
   As yet steam's iron giant rushed not here ;
Many a long league through Cornwall must be traced
   Ere they could win the goal of hope yet fear.
They recked not rocks or streams, but o'er them swept,
They flew past cottages where labour slept ;
They flew past Druid stone and Danish round,
Startling the calm with lash and clattering bound.

"The dawn !" Tresillian cried ; "it breaks too soon ;
   On, Pender, on ! a rich reward is thine,
Reach we in time "— Just then the paling moon
   Went down behind the bare hills' granite line,
And amber-streaks shot up heaven's eastern wall,
Night drawing slowly back her ebon pall ;
Swiftly they sped, the early miner passed,
But on the wild-browed man no glance they cast.

The steeds breathed hard, their eye-balls strained in pain,
  The generous brutes, exhausted, checked their pace;
Oh, must they sink, the riders' efforts vain,
  No other steeds in that lone desert place?
The men, dismounting at a runnel's brink,
Washed their hot coursers' sides, and gave them drink,
With wheaten biscuit, for themselves designed,
Tapping and stroking them, with coaxings kind.

Refreshed, again the horses pawed the ground,
  And westward flew, like meteors, down the moor;
The gale brought vigour, and, with livelier bound,
  Brook or obstructing bank they vaulted o'er.
Hark! fainter in the distance hoofs are heard,
Each steed grows small, like some dim-flying bird,
Now disappears—on, on, ye spirits brave!
Oh, will Tresillian reach in time to save?

———————

Morn woke up cheerily with laughing skies,
  The rooks cawed out, clouds rosier seemed to float,
Flowers in the garden spread their richest dyes,
  The blackbird's bill poured forth its mellowest note:
The sun drank all the dew-tears in the grass,
Where freshened kingcups waved, a golden mass;
Billows danced shoreward with a glittering sheen;
Nought, breathing pain or sorrow, marked the scene.

K

Then in the mansion women early rose,
　A bustle spread from chamber unto hall;
Bouquets are meant for joy, not twined for woes;
　Old servants' feet more lightly seemed to fall;
Like wind-kissed lilies or new wreaths of snow,
The active bridesmaids fluttered to and fro;
All kindly aided, every heart was gay,
Young, old, rejoiced on Sibyl's nuptial day.

She, too, was early up, and busy hands
　Soon dressed her in the vestments of a bride—
The orange-wreath, the milk-soft pearly bands,
　The robe of virgin whiteness, floating wide;
She yielded passively; they did not know
Her quivering lip, pale cheek, betokened woe,
But thought, as brides will tremble, that the hour
Touched her young spirit with its wonted power.

And beautiful she looked; her dark-brown hair
　Affluent, with whitest blossoms intertwined,
Was rolled in shining volumes, her sweet air
　More sweet and witching for a saddened mind:
Her stag-like eyes, which checked their sunny flashes,
Drooped tenderly beneath their silken lashes;
A tear, the dew of feeling, on her cheek,
She looked a young Madonna, bright yet meek.

A moment Sibyl prayed to be alone;
  Then sorrow bore her down, and claimed its sway;
She viewed her bridal dress with bursting moan,
  Longing to rend the glittering pearls away,
And from her brow that orange-wreath to tear,
Such gorgeous show but mocking her despair;
Sackcloth should rather clothe her, and dun night
Wrap her in gloom—Oh, sad, unwelcome light!

The fatal time was come, no power might shun;
  She could not now rebel, or ward the dart;
They thought her happiest maid beneath the sun—
  Oh, anguish, anguish of a breaking heart!
He wandered far away, but still all truth,
The dear-loved plighted one of early youth;
Yet duty bowed his will, she too must bow,
Nor strive with fate, all useless misery now.

She pressed her white hands o'er her whiter face,
  And through the fingers tears were trickling slow,
Like dew down morning lilies; you might trace
  The strength of anguish in their bitter flow;
But soon she calmed her feelings' outward storm,
Just rocking to and fro her stooping form,
While with her tremulous foot she beat the floor—
Poor foot to lightsome thoughts to trip no more.

K 2

See her upon her knees, with hands raised high
  Above her lovely head, beseeching heaven
To grant her strength, that this last agony
  Might pass away, and inward peace be given!
So soft her prayer, her breathings were unheard,
But her torn breast through all its depths was stirred;
God, hear that stricken one, and balm impart,
And to the trial nerve her shrinking heart!

A step—her father came; she reached her seat;
  She would not pain him by that grief's display;
Dear, tender hypocrite, a smile most sweet
  O'erspread her face while dashing tears away;
He viewed her wistfully—" For me, for me,
All this is done—God's blessing rest on thee!
My duteous, sacrificed, unselfish child!"
And still she kissed his hands, looked up, and smiled.

But now the veil the maidens o'er her threw,
  The nuptial badge sure wrought by fairy fingers;
It floated like a cloud the moon looks through,
  When near her orb its wreath of silver lingers:
Yet the transparent lace less white appeared
Than those white shoulders, which their marble reared—
Than that fair forehead smoothed by seeming gladness,
The heart the while despondency and sadness.

The martyr goeth to the stake, to die
  Calmly for creeds his lip will not gainsay;
Sibyl the chariot entered with no sigh,
  And tow'rd the church they slowly took their way:
That hawthorn-lane which every shrub endears,
She oft had tripped along in childhood's years;
Her next walk there, her heart would drag a chain,
To break whose links dumb grief must strive in vain.

By those green elms Tresillian spoke of love;
  O Memory, close your wounds! heart, hush your
    sighs!
The dream is over—dead, joy's stricken dove;
  To think what might have been—there torture lies.
They reached the village, where so oft her hand
Had scattered alms; the simple rustic band
Stood in their doorways now, fond glances cast,
And bared their heads, and cheered her as she passed.

They reached the ancient church; the ivied pile
  Stately its crown of ages strove to wear;
Through all its solemn moss it seemed to smile
  Down on the crowd so blithely gathered there;
All gay save two, whom grief's dark arms embraced,
And on whose suffering hearts a load was placed,
Weighty enough, though firm that load they bore,
To crush out hope and bliss for evermore.

The white-drest peasant-maids were grouping round,
   Holding their willow-baskets heaped with flowers,
Ready, the rite performed, to strew the ground—
   Ready to cry—long life, and happy hours!
And·there the lusty ringers were preparing,
Uncoiling the strong ropes, their stout arms baring,
To send ere long, o'er echoing mount and dell,
A joyous peal for her all loved so well.

The nuptial party tow'rd the altar passed;
   Sibyl turned white as ashes, and her eyes,
Painfully restless, piteous glances cast,
   Her bosom struggling with its agonies.
She sobbed, seemed choking, and her limbs all shook,
But, raising to her father one quick look,
Her strength returned; she faintly smiled, and then
Lifted her head, nor shrank, nor sobbed again.

Osborne stood waiting at the altar rail,
   Sternly determined, but with placid mien;
And Sibyl forward stepped, composed though pale,
   The bridesmaids, like white clouds, behind her seen:
And many circled near, their eyes all bent
On one fair object, while, in flashes sent,
Rich purple rays through pictured windows streamed,
And, like a quivering glory, o'er them beamed.

The priest unclosed his book; a pause like death,
  An ominous chill around appeared to fall—
A creeping chill that made each hold his breath,
  As if some wrong were done, though veiled from all:
Osborne, impatient, chid the unmeet delay,
Yet still they paused, while plainly, far away,
They heard the river's flow—then on the ear
Broke tramp of steeds, that drew more near, and near.

The priest had now begun; all hushed remained;
  The solemn words were read, unwavering, slow;
An instant more the steeds the porch had gained,
  And eager voices mixed with murmurs low;
Then burst a shout—two men by travel worn,
Heads bare, white faces, garments soiled and torn,
Entered, despite the crowd, the holy pile,
And rushed, in frantic haste, along the aisle.

There are some scenes weak words can ne'er portray;
  As well attempt to paint a flash of light;
Leave them to vivid fancy, whose full ray,
  Beyond all art, can make the picture bright:
The nuptial party stood in wild surprise,
Some turned inquiringly, with angry eyes;
The rite unsaid, Trelawn had dropped his book,
Fear in his heart, and wonder in his look.

"'Tis he! he lives!" the pastor breathless cried;
   He clasped his hands; his tongue could speak no more;
Trembling he leant against the altar's side,
   Then slowly sank, as sense and life were o'er.
Tresillian stood erect, on Osborne gazed,
One hand on Pender, while his keen eyes blazed;
"Yes, he doth live!—the truth thou knewest well,
And now let conscience be thy scourge—thy hell!"

But Pender raised Trelawn, and kindly spoke;
   He knew how great his grief for many a year;
All his revenge should be—his heart, though oak,
   Had softest spots—to wipe the good man's tear.
Thrice happy now Trelawn, the hideous stain
Of murder gone, removed his load of pain!
Now might he preach, and calm in spirit pray,
And guide the wanderer on his heavenly way.

And how did Sibyl bear this wildering hour?
   Amazement seized her soul, but flooding all
First strong emotions, joy had strongest power;
   The fetters of long misery seemed to fall.
Not for herself, but father, warmest bliss
Poured on her spirit; from a dark abyss
His age was snatched, and well she might rejoice,
Striving to speak, but feeling choked her voice.

Her arms were round him flung, her face upraised
  Looking into his own, and kisses wild
Were printed on his cheek; she gazed and gazed
  Through blinding tears, and then her sweet lips
    smiled:
What recked that maid the silent wonderers there,
Deeming her frenzied by that look and air?
And while fond rapture still her bosom stirred,
Sibyl her father clasped, but spoke no word.

She moved his white hair gently from his brow,
  And kissed once more his cheeks and brightened eyes,
Paused to collect her thoughts, and, grateful now,
  Looked up to heaven with tears, and smiles, and sighs:
Such gestures are soul's language, when the heart
Fails through the lips its feelings to impart;
At length she cried—" Thy sorrows now are o'er,
Kneel, pray with me ! none, none can wrong thee more!"

Then did Tresillian, in brief words, unfold
  All that to those around mysterious seemed ;
And Osborne knew—truth's dreaded story told—
  Vainly his craft had duped, his brain had schemed:
Sullen he left the church, bowed low his pride,
Glad in obscurity his head to hide ;
He gave no challenge, and he urged no love ;
Villains, detected, ever cowards prove.

Sibyl, more calm, around bright glances cast,
 And, moving forward from her father's arms,
Stood 'mid the group, all fear, all sadness past,
 Unveiled, yet radiant in her bridal charms;
Tresillian took her hand, she hung her head,
One burning blush from cheek to forehead spread;
They loved in childhood, and, through good and ill,
All saw and felt they loved each other still.

Autumn was sleeping on the thankful earth,
 The fruits were hanging ripened on the tree,
From field and orchard swelled the voice of mirth—
 The harvest-time—dear hours of jollity!
The rose her last sweets hastened to unfold,
The woods were mantled all in cloaks of gold;
Bees with their last rich gatherings humm'd along,
And piped the thrush his farewell, plaintive song.

The saffron beams, as day's god sought his pillow,
  Mellowed and sobered, were serenely cast
On that small garden by the western billow,
  Where Sibyl's childhood, nursed 'mid flowers, was
      past;
The quivering ray soft kissed an aged cheek,
While joy from each lined feature strove to speak;
His eye now sought the glory-curtained west,
Then on some dearer object loved to rest.

Trelawn was happy now, to feel no more
  Conscience' sharp pang, or mourn a daughter's woes;
Earth was content with Autumn's gathered store,
  So, like the year, his ripened age would close.
He raised his hands unconsciously, a prayer
His lips were breathing for a wedded pair,
That heaven each blessing on their lives would shower,
Turning to rapture trial's bitter hour.

They sat beneath ancestral, spreading trees,
  The far church-tower was bathed in amber light,
And bells were sprinkling music on the breeze,
  Whispering in Nature's ear—good night, good night!
Tresillian thought if raptures that belong
To restless life, in pleasure's brilliant throng,
Eclipsed the joys that here in calm might flow—
He looked on Sibyl, and love answered—no!

She only clasped his hand, and watched his eyes,
   Blessing the scene, the hour, the sun that passed
To glorious rest, and those o'erruling skies
   That, showering mercies, gave them joy at last.
For him she'd live, and, like lens-gathered beams,
In him would centre all her hopes and dreams,
And time on earth, and endless years above,
Should not exhaust, but only strengthen love.

THE END.

THE LAND'S END:

ST. MICHAEL'S MOUNT:

AND

MISCELLANEOUS POEMS.

THE LAND'S END.

WHAT are Rome's ruins, moss-grown, rent, and gray
What Baalbec's fanes majestic in decay?
What the huge pyramids that stand sublime,
Defying earthquakes and the scythe of Time?
   To Nature's ruins towering here—
     Ruins in awful wildness hurled,
    Great God-built pyramids that rear
    Their crests through earth's eternal year,
     Like relics of some darker world?

Bolerium!* cape of storms! strong buttress raised
By Britain's genius, as she sternly gazed
Tow'rd the blue distant west, resolved to wage
Unceasing battle with mad ocean's rage;
    Pillars of granite! fanes of rock!
    Braving the blasting lightning-shock,

* The classic name of the Land's End.

Scowling in grimness o'er the sea,
Furrowed by tempests, as they sweep
Through wave-worn arch and gallery deep—
    The tempests of eternity!
Giants in stone, that cry aloud
To the first billow, first wild cloud,
    Reaching Britannia's shore—
" This is the land where power is dwelling,
Where freedom smiles, and fame is telling
    Her golden story evermore !"

The soul is awed upon this granite tower ;
  Gazing from toppling crags so wild and lone,
Uppiled, methinks, by some enchanter's power,
  Terror's storm-girded throne—
Gazing on seething, thundering waves below,
Till the heart quakes, the eyes all dizzy grow :
    The waves that onward roll and flash,
    Shaking the huge rocks with their dash,
    From granite bounds again recoiling,
    In broken masses, foaming, boiling—
    The waves that, in those cavern-halls,
    Sound like a thousand waterfalls,
    Or deep-mouthed trumpets, pouring proud
    Their boisterous music long and loud—
    Those awful piles of living stone,
    Savage, majestic, and alone,

Traced o'er with lines that odes may be,
Not penned by children of the sod,
But poems of sublimity,
Writ by the hand of storms and God—
We well may yield to solemn, lofty thought;
How small the change long ages here have wrought!
We muse and sigh—how brief are mortal hours!
What dust is man! how puny all his powers!

But now a calm comes down, and lulls the roar,
And soothes the ocean-lion into sleep;
The waves in wrath no longer lash the shore,
Or, like white chargers, sweep:
The sun hangs mellow in the burnished west,
And painted crags reflect his mild farewell;
The sea-mew, landward wheeling, seeks her nest,
And ocean's organ peals with gentler swell.
Wide-scattering surf is turned to dust of gold,
The Lady-Rock* is blushing ruby-red,
The little sea-pink, in her craggy hold,
Shuts her blue eye, and bows her sleepy head.

---

* The "Irish Lady," or the "Lady-Rock," stands near the coast, and derives its singular name from a legend that the ghost of a lady, who was wrecked here on her passage from Ireland, is frequently seen on the summit of the crag during storms.

The last rich odours from the heath arise,
Offerings from those wild altars to the skies :
The friendly Longships,* from its foam-bound site,
Smiles o'er the surge in that soft, tranquil light,
And soon begins to trick its own red ray,
To warn from rocks, and point the seaman's way.
Peace walks the deep, and stills the purple air,
And Nature folds her hands as if in prayer;
Beauty heaven-sent, sublimity profound,
Fall, like an angel's mantle, softly round;
God's works, not man's, claim reverence, love, and fear,
His mighty presence only reigning here.

---

* The Longships Lighthouse crowns a rock about one mile
and a half from the shore; and the lantern, though 127 feet
above low water mark, is frequently in winter covered with
waves and foam, while all communication with the land is
cut off.

ST. MICHAEL'S MOUNT,
CORNWALL.

FAMED Mount, that risest from the western deep,
  With granite shoulders and fern-waving hair,
Like some tall giant doomed sea-watch to keep,
  Spoken to stone, and fixed for ever there !

Or thou dost look, so beautiful, while grand,
  Wooing the gales, and towering o'er the foam,
An islet of enchantment, where a band ,
  Of ocean-nymphs, and mermaids, make their home.

I cross the pebbly ridge, where, long ago,
  Ere Christ was born, the old Phœnicians trod,
Bearing their precious store ;* wild ocean's flow
  Sounds now, as then, loud anthems unto God.

* Twice a day, at low water, the visitor can pass to St. Michael's Mount dry-shod. Across this periodic isthmus, the Phœnicians transported the tin obtained from the Britons, making the Mount a kind of depôt for the metal. This renowned and romantic pile of rocks is nearly a mile in circumference, and has an elevation of more than 200 feet above the sand.

The sun smiles out; I climb the massive rocks
 Smoothed by the blasts of ages, and in dread
Hang o'er the billow-lashed, huge, granite blocks;
 Soul feeds upon the grandeur round her spread.

Yet here the lichen, creeping, loving, grows,
 And in the chinks the heath-flower swings its bell ;
The wandering bee her shrilly trumpet blows,
 Heard in the pauses of blue ocean's swell.

Loneness doth kiss her sister Quiet's brow;
 Amid the ferns the timid rabbit feeds,
And on the iron cannon, rusting now,
 The linnet carols, nor my footstep heeds.

I reach the craggy summit, seaward gazing;
 O Bay of beauty ! green encircling hills !
O sun upon the crystal waters blazing,
 Each wave a cup that liquid emerald fills !

Capes stretch away, and woo the outer deep,
 And one is lost in haze,* like memory dying
And fading in the past; ships onward sweep,
 And some are idly at their anchors lying :

---

* The Lizard Point.

Lying on moving glass, where each white sail
    Is traced in shadow; hark! the organ's sound!*
It mingles with the sea-mew's fitful wail,
    And chime of bells from distant towers around.

Here captive Beauty mourned her absent lord,
    Watching and weeping as the sun went down;
She sighed his name—wild waves an answer roared,
    That name more dear than splendour or a crown.†

The monks sang anthems on this sacred steep,‡
    Their vespers seaward floating, dying, swelling;
Here 'mid the beautiful their ashes sleep;
    Nought of their story now the winds are telling.

---

* The chapel on the summit of the Mount contains a fine organ. At one of the angles of the tower, and very difficult to be reached, is the famous *St. Michael's chair*, the old legend attached to the latter being, that whichever of a newly-married couple first contrives to sit in this chair, he or she will maintain the mastery over the other for life.

† Lady Catherine Gordon, wife of Perkin Warbeck, the pretender to the crown of England in the reign of Henry VII., was held prisoner for some time at the Mount.

‡ Edward the Confessor founded the priory of Benedictine monks on St. Michael's Mount. Many interesting objects of antiquity are preserved in the venerable building, and the old

And here, in recent day, did Britain's queen
   Stand on the rocks—a throne, a throne sublime !
And Cornwall's duke gazed raptured on the scene;
   Their names the Mount shall keep all future time.*

The waves beneath are ever rolling, beating,
   Their ceaseless voice a mournful monotone;
Slow they advance, again in foam retreating;
   Great Ocean's heart, why dost thou ever moan ?

St. Michael's Mount ! who gazes from this height,
   On loveliness, sublimity, and peace,
On Nature in a trance of full delight—
   Nature whose glories ne'er shall dim or cease :

Will feel an inward fire unfelt before,
   The glow of admiration, and will muse
On Him who shaped far hills and winding shore,
   The sea, the sky, with all their varied hues.

refectory of the monks has obtained the name of the Chevy-
Chase-room, from its singularly ornamented freize.'

  * Her Majesty Queen Victoria and the Prince Consort visited
St. Michael's Mount in the autumn of 1846. A brass plate, the
shape of the Queen's foot, has been inserted in one of the stones
of the small pier where she landed. The visit of the Prince and
Princess of Wales took place in July, 1865.

Oh, yes, our spirits to exalt and please,
  God hath indulged choice dreams of beauty here,
And stamped them on creation ; scenes like these
  Reflect heaven's love, and glorify our sphere.

THE SEASON OF YOUTH.
AN ODE.

YOUTH, sweet maiden youth !
When time flies with angel-wings,
And gush brightly fancy's springs ;
Jubilant hour of body's health,
Strength and freshness passing wealth ;
When the step is fairy lightness,
And the eyes are dewy brightness—
Eyes, the gay soul's starry dwelling,
    Ever sparkling,
    Never darkling,
Still of hope and pleasure telling.
When the brow no care discloses,
And the cheeks are softest roses,
Where the dimple plays for ever,
But sad tears will wander never ;

When the lip so wreathed and merry,
In its redness mocks the cherry,
And the hair, so glossy, bright,
Shineth like a crown of light,
Or in rolled-up mass appears,
No grey line betraying years;
Oh, delightful, maiden youth!
   Time to return no more,
   With its rich golden store,
Thrice happy, envied youth!

Beautiful season of glad dreams!
When the far-beckoning future seems
Not dark and lowering, but with sky
  Softly cerulean, with a bow
In every cloud, and still on high
  A sun with summer-glow:
When, in the opening path of life,
Bristles no thorn of woe or strife,
  But roses strew the way,
  The vista green and gay,
With music of hope's birds for ever ringing,
And fancy's fairies sweetly singing,
While pleasures on each side, with radiant eyes,
Promise á lasting paradise.

Youth, enchanting youth!
All-to-gold transmuting youth!

No thoughts of coming leaden years,
Of trials, hard experience, tears,
Entering the palace of the brain,
That airy, happy, bright domain.
Dear spring-time of the soul, all joy and bloom!
Youth, heeding not far age's cold and gloom,
Feasting on delicate and odorous flowers,
That deck warm life's luxurious bowers!
Youth, buoyant-hearted youth!

Time to return no more,
With its rich golden store,

Oh, happy, blessèd youth!

Maiden, with the beaming face,
Laughing eyes, and form of grace,
On whose lip no sigh is heard,
Blithesome as an April bird,
Moving in the glittering dance,

Like a white cloud, to and fro,

With good temper in each glance,

With thy young cheeks all a-glow;

I do blame thee not, fair creature;
When I view each lovely feature,

When I see the joys that rise,
Sparkling in thy violet eyes,
Heightening all thy budding charms,
Leaning thus in pleasure's arms,
I but think of that bright day,
When my soul, like thine, was gay;
I but blessings breathe upon thee;
May Time's hand rest lightly on thee!
May no grief heart's blossoms blight!
Mayst thou draw from love delight!
Take thy guileless pastimes now,
While youth's roses deck thy brow;
Grace, and beauty that endears,
Oft will crown maturer years,
Yet, back-gazing, still I cry,
As the joy-winged moments fly—
Envied season, hopeful youth !
    Time to return no more,
    With its rich golden store,
O happy, blessèd youth !

THE EVENING OF LIFE.

Oft, after storms, ere Nature drops to sleep,
  What beauty sunset brings,
Crowning with saintly halos every steep,
  Peace spreading wide her wings!

Such is life's closing hour; the tranquil scene,
  After dark trials, bright—
An hour oft beautiful, and oft serene
  With mind's rich, mellowing light.

Youth, with the airy step and frolic eye,
  Smooth brow, and cheek of bloom!
Dread not the time when these prized charms must fly,
  Think not calm age is gloom.

What though your glossy black or sunny hair
  Be streaked ere long with white,
Think not the soul will shine less proud or fair;
  For soul there comes no night.

Age, dear, expected haven of sweet rest,
    Crossed the wild seas of life!
Close of a war, when passions in the breast
    Lay by their arms of strife!

Blest season, when the soul mild thoughts will send,
    Like doves, through earth and sky,
Action's strong flood subsided; when we end
    Harsh thoughts in harmony.

Yes, farewell music from wide Nature peals,
    Sweet to reflective hearts;
So richer glory o'er life's landscape steals,
    As the warm beam departs.

Fond recollections cast their mellow haze
    O'er hours of joy gone by;
The soul feels pleasure backward still to gaze,
    Though she may pause to sigh.

Oh, many the delights that wait on age,
    Unknown to earlier years!
Leisure to counsel youth, con wisdom's page,
    And wipe pale Sorrow's tears.

In our arm-chair by book-lore we can roam,
  View earth with fancy's eyes ;
And we can hear the songs of love and home,
  Murmuring of paradise.

Blest hour, when soul is peace, hopes lure no more,
  Calm resignation given;
'Tis as a bridge of gold, life's trials o'er,
  Passing us on to heaven.

THE DREAM OF THE LONDON SEAMSTRESS.

Heavy, and slow, and booming loud,
  St. Paul's has struck the midnight hour; ·
A fog comes down, and in its shroud
  Wraps street, and bridge, and tower:
The gas-lamp struggles through the gloom,
Men walk, as in a murky tomb;
While falls the chilly, drizzling rain,
      Beading each pane.

High in a garret, lone and small,
  Her only wealth—bed, table, chair,
Silent she works; no tear-drops fall,
  For she has learnt to bear;
Has learnt to smother struggling sorrow,
And ceased to gild with hope life's morrow;
Though gone her strength, and lost her bloom,
        Work is her doom.

Hour after hour she plies her fingers;
  Two—three, St. Paul's has sounded deep;
Her head droops low, her quick hand lingers—
  She starts—she must not sleep:
She hums a tune; again her eyes
Close, like two flowers 'neath evening's skies;
Down on her work her head is cast,
        She sleeps at last.

O dreams, restorer of joy's gold
  To bankrupt hearts! kind, blessèd dreams!
No rain, no night, she doth behold—
  A summer morning beams;
A country cottage 'mid sweet bowers,
Bees humming round rich-scented flowers,
A brawling brook, and, far away,
        The cuckoo's lay.

Her youthful sisters' voices sound,
   Her father, living, talks and smiles;
The Sabbath-bell now murmurs 'round,
   They cross the fields and ancient stiles;
Ruff'd daisies make the pathway fair,
The clover scents the sunny air;
Her heart, like earth in beauty clad,
      Is gay and glad.

She seems within the church to stand,
   Sees font and pulpit's quaint-carved dove,
The white-robed pastor, and the band
   Of rustic singers ranged above:
The prayer is breathed; she kneels and sighs,
And to her Maker lifts her eyes;
The choir breaks out, the old wall shakes;
      She starts and wakes.

She wakes—where church, where suns that glow?
   The dreary night, the drizzling rain,
The candle in its socket low—
   She wakes to truth and pain.
O happy days flashed back in sleep!
Their light makes darkness now more deep;
And while she blesses earlier years,
      She yields to tears.

She weeps, and works amid her sorrow,
    And those she toils for sleep the while;
Will better fortune bless to-morrow?
    Can hope her heart beguile?
Yes, hope of that far land of peace,
Where hunger gnaws not, toils will cease,
And tears, life's bitter struggles o'er,
            Shall flow no more.

WOMAN'S LOVE.

As Spring, blithe maiden, tripping soft and light,
    With happy, beaming eyes,
Doth cold and sullen Winter put to flight,
    And cheer all earth and skies;
So woman's love makes warm man's frigid heart,
Bidding his moody dreams and gloom depart.

As Summer sports in rich, luxurious bowers,
    Her cheeks all rosy mirth,
Scatters on every bank delicious flowers,
    And beautifies the earth;
So woman's smile our brightened homes will bless,
Making life gay with flowers of loveliness.

As teeming Autumn yields her precious store,
    Ripe fruits and bending corn,
Heaping abundance, till, for flowing o'er,
    She scarce can hold her horn;
So woman's love a wealth of joy will yield,
All heart-fruits gathered from that fertile field.

Without yon sun—kind source of heat and light,
    What were the earth we boast?
An orphan thing, wide wrapt in frost and night,
    A sad world's wandering ghost;
So man cold, dark, and cheerlessly would move
Along life's path, bereft of woman's love.

As the chaste lady moon, with brow serene,
    Climbing the stormy sky,
Soon spreads her calming silver o'er the scene,
    And bids the dark clouds fly;
So woman's love sweet influence sheds on life,
Brightens its gloom, and stills the storms of strife.

M

As gold, hot-glowing in the furnace-flame,
     Defies heat's wasting might,
And, unconsumed, doth issue forth the same,
     Only more pure and bright;
So 'mid fierce trials true love ne'er expires,
Made purer by affliction's searching fires.

In the great tune of being, discords oft
     The warring passions raise,
But there's a harmony which, sweet and soft,
     Tempers the jarring lays;
'Tis woman's love, for harshness sweetness grows,
Where that subduing, dulcet music flows.

As mosses weave a beauty 'round decay,
     Hiding the rents of years,
Till on the mournful ruin, worn and gray,
     A gentle smile appears;
So woman's love gives beauty and a grace
To poverty's poor, shattered dwelling-place.

The purest fount of joy, the tenderest light
     Cheering the heart of woe,
Lending to strength a softness, weakness might,
     Heaven's choicest gift below,
The comforter in sickness, still above
Owning its source—such, such is woman's love.

HYMN TO THE RISING SUN.

———

Hail! Bridegroom of creation, never old!
Shake off thy sleep, thy curtained brow unfold,
Put on thy vests of purple and of gold.

Rise from thy couch behind the orient hill,
Shoot thy beam-shafts, and heaven with splendour fill,
A god, a god, in power and beauty still!

Ocean beholds thee, and affrighted night
Flies the blue waves, the sands turn jewels bright,
The billows sparkling, leaping in delight.

The vales and mountains, welcome! welcome! cry,
To see thee like a giant climb the sky,
Vigour and life wide-flashing from thine eye.

Man's sense rejoices, and his frame acquires
New freshness, strength, with thy rekindled fires,
And grateful soul in sympathy aspires.

All Nature feels thy influence, king of light!
Each beam a blessing, whether flashed in might,
Or gently stealing down the infinite.

The little flower, that all the night had kept
Its petals closed, and in chill shadow slept,
Moist with the tears its eyes of beauty wept;

Thrilled by the ardour of thy piercing ray,
Expands its bosom, shakes grief-drops away,
And laughs in joy to front the jocund day.

Thy beams reach tenderly the lark's low nest,
Where 'neath the stars soft mosses he had prest;
Opening his diamond eye, he starts from rest.

Up like a mounting thought, his winglets bear
His small brown form to heaven, and, quivering there,
He rains down music through the glowing air.

O sun! there's nothing, in wide earth or sky,
But blesses thee; thou wakest, far and nigh,
The eternal chords of golden harmony.

Hail! world-reviving, all-embracing sphere!
Burning but unconsumed, thy great career
Passing in splendour all things splendid here.

How terrible yet beautiful art thou,
Power throned on thy unchanging, radiant brow,
To which the circling worlds obedient bow!

Great minister of God! mysterious sun!
Will e'er thy beams die out, thy mission done?
Will the worlds need thee, when Time's course is run?

We know not, burning glory! what thy doom,
Yet reft of thee, yon skies to us were gloom,
And death would turn quick Nature to a tomb.

Then hail, thrice hail! thou eldest born of Time,
Walking the heavens as in thy joyous prime,
Fountain of life! God's emblem most sublime!

Dispensing good, still in our centre blaze!
Let glad creation, basking in thy rays,
Clap her exulting hands, and hymn thy praise.

OCEAN'S CHANGES.

Gentle deep!
With thy placid, shining breast,
Like an infant's taking rest,
In the cradle of the world;
When each little wave is curled,
Like the locks which, smooth and bright,
Deck that infant's brow of light.
When along the burnished tide,
White-winged vessels mirrored glide,
And the clouds, small fleeces, glow
On the emerald fields below,
Lambs of heaven, like softest snow.

Merry deep!
When morn's sparkle on thee lies,
Bright as flash in beauty's eyes,
As all frolic, joy, she seems
Waking up from blissful dreams;

When thy waves on pebbles bound,
With a running silvery sound,
Bubbling music at our feet,
Like young laughter soft and sweet.

Mournful deep !
With night's shadows coming down,
Nature's wide-spread, silent frown,
Stars upon thee dimly shining ;
Mighty monster, still repining,
In thy pain and dark unrest,
Something locked in thy great breast,
Breathing of deep sadness,
Banishing our gladness ;
With most mournful kisses,
Lips that give no blisses,
Moaning on the glimmering shore,
In a sullen, under roar ;
Waves still heaving, ever breaking,
A mysterious language speaking.
Oh, melancholy-sounding sea !
A hollow voice from past eternity,
Telling us of the years for ever fled,
Like a great bell deep-tolling in thy bed,
Along the depths slow-swinging, booming, sighing,
For something in surrounding Nature dying ;

What dies we nought may know, yet to our souls
Sadly that fancied bell for ever tolls.

Cruel deep!
When the storm his vengeance takes,
Thy mad passion too awakes;
Then no fury from below,
Bent on spreading death and woe,
Fiery scorpions round her brow,
Is more terrible than thou.
See! thy waves are raging, roaring,
Eager round the vessel pouring;
Now upswelling like a mountain,
Boiling now like some vast fountain,
Opening then as if to swallow,
In that whirling, ghastly hollow,
Poor humanity that shivers,
As the doomed ship rocks and quivers—
Quivers, trembling, plunging, reeling,
Quivers as instinct with feeling.
Now thou send'st that bark on high,
   Now into the white abyss,
Mocking seamen's agony,
   With thy fiendish hiss.
Prayers to thee are no avail,
Nought thou heed'st the victim's wail

Down to gulfs, down whirling, where
Death is sitting with despair;
Down from daylight into dark,
Watched by horror, sinks the bark:
Swells one thrilling, drowning cry,
Then the billows leap on high,
Fierce exulting as they boom
O'er the seaman's stormy tomb.—
Hungry, pitiless, murderous sea!
Oh, what wild shrieks hath terror sent o'er thee!
How many millions, dead,
Lie waiting in thy oozy bed,
Till the last trumpet sound, and death no more
Shall revel mid thy rage, and maddening roar!

FRENCH AND ENGLISH BEAUTIES.

TRIPPING gently, tripping lightly,
With small foot that wakes no sound;
Glancing keenly, glancing brightly,
On each dear-loved object round.

Figure slender, jetty tresses
   Fillets might be proud to bind ;
Eye that sparkles, and expresses
   All the active, joyous mind.

At the shrine of pleasure kneeling,
   Reckless of the future years,
For the moment deeply feeling,
   But soon dashing off her tears.

Pleased with all things, talking, smiling,
   Cheerful star 'mid sorrow's night,
From her bosom care exiling,
   Mere existence a delight.

With no deep thoughts spirit-laden,
   Yet most rich in fancy's fire ;
Such is Gallia's light-souled maiden ;
   Praise her, love her, and admire.

Saxon beauty ! on my dreaming,
   Pensive, radiant vision, rise !
Moving proudly, yet still seeming
   Mild of mien, with love-soft eyes.

There she leans—faint-blushing roses,
  Softest hues from morning caught,
Tint her cheek, where calm reposes;
  Smooth that brow, the throne of thought.

Plainly classic, richly shining,
  Back is drawn the dark-brown hair;
As the moon, with silver lining,
  Makes at eve fair clouds more fair;

So the soul doth fling more brightness
  On the form already bright;
Beauty, graceful in its lightness,
  Winning, growing on the sight.

With the statue's fine ideal,
  Carved by matchless Grecian skill,
She doth mingle all the real,
  Warmer, but as perfect still.

Sunny as the heavens above her,
  Looking virtue, shine her eyes,
Spirit's home; who would not love her,
  And that English beauty prize?

Truth, affection, and deep feeling,
  Nestle, dove-like, in her breast;
Guardian angels! round her stealing,
  Watch her, guide her, make her blest!

SOLITARY CONFINEMENT.

Ye who gaze on God's blue sky,
  Walk the meadows, scent the flowers,
Cannot grasp the agony,
  E'en in thought, of my past hours—
Lonely, lonely, all alone,
  With no human voice, no sound,
Pent within damp walls of stone,
  All my world that narrow bound—
Oh, the horror who can tell,
Of the solitary cell?

Night might fall, or day might waken,
  Day and night the same to me;
Were my cell by earthquake shaken,
  That at least some change would be:

But my lot was changeless ever,
　　Nought to mark slow time I knew—
One Dead Sea where breezes never
　　O'er the poisoned waters blew :
Oh, the sadness who may tell
Of the lonely, silent cell ?

How I've longed to see the features
　　Of home's darlings, none may know ;
E'en one word from human creatures
　　Would have soothed my pining woe ;
But no face—no voice—no greeting—
　　Silent, lonely, still alone ;
Souls were made for social meeting,
　　Hearts, though erring, are not stone :
Oh, the misery who may tell
Of the solitary cell ?

Pacing, pacing, to and fro,
　　Now across and back again ;
Gazing upward, then below,
　　Like a tiger in his den ;
With no book to please or cheer me,
　　Feeding on my own sad heart,
Sometimes fancying people near me,
　　Weeping as their shades depart :

Oh, the horror who may tell
Of the lonely, silent cell?

When, out-worn, deep sleep has bound me,
  Free again I've roved in dreams,
Hills, and vales, and flowers around me,
  Basking in the sun's glad beams;
Friends, wife, children! tarry longer!
  But the happy dream would flee,
And I'd wake with anguish stronger,
  No one there, save grief and me:
Oh, the torment who may tell
Of that lonely, silent cell?

Give me labour, crushing, weary;
  Give me stripes—I'll calmly bear;
But the long hours, dark and dreary,
  And the stillness—torture there!
Memory's burden, brooding sadness—
  Living inly, and yet dead—
Thoughts that pierce and turn to madness,
  Days of languor, nights of dread:
Oh, the horror who may tell
Of the lonely, silent cell?

THE VAGRANT'S CHILD.

Thou little child in rags—
Hanging at thy mother's side,
  Sullen, moping, weeping,
What to thee all London's pride,
  O'er the pavement creeping,
Asking alms of passers-by,
Tears for ever in thine eye?

Thou little child in rags—
Pattering on with naked feet,
  Hungry, wretched, shivering,
Like a blot upon the street,
  Little red lip quivering;
Looking through the shop's great pane,
At delicious food in vain.

Thou little child in rags—
With thy uncut, jetty hair,
  To thy shoulders streaming,
With thy forehead bold and fair,
  With thy great eyes beaming,
With thy young mind like a star
Hidden by thick clouds afar.

Thou little child in rags—
I do follow thee with sighs,
  By thy half-inebriate mother,
Fearing her stern-flashing eyes,
  Trying sobs to smother—
Beaten, chid, through good and ill
Clinging to her garments still.

Thou little child in rags—
This is destiny, or fate;
  Dark enigma! wondrous heaven!
Wert thou born in other state,
  What to thee perchance were given?
Gayest dress, toys, sweetest kisses,
Maids to wait—a world of blisses.

Thou little child in rags—
Yes, thou mightst have been the heir
　To some dukedom great and old,
Or one day a crown mightst wear,
　And a sceptre hold;
Or a general thou mightst be,
Shouting freedom, victory!

Thou little child in rags—
Fortune might have placed thee near
　Learning's temple, and thy mind
Might be destined, with each year,
　Some immortal truth to find;
Like a Newton, worlds exploring,
Or a Milton, heavenward soaring.

Thou little child in rags—
Now, I fear me, thou wilt grow
　To a lawless, reckless man,
Stealing, working others' woe,
　Punished, ever under ban;
But I pray thou ne'er mayst be
Led unto the gallows-tree.

Thou little child in rags—
  Hanging at thy mother's side,
    Sullen, moping, weeping,
What to thee all London's pride,
    O'er the pavement creeping?
Still in penury thou wilt roam,
Through the world without a home.

THE CLASSIC RHONE.

No more a hundred temples gleam
  Along thy banks, bright, arrowy Rhone!
The Cæsars' pomp is but a dream,
  The Goth and Vandal long have flown;
No more the notes of harp and flute
  Sound from the Pagan's pillar'd shrine,
The Dryads' prophet-oak is mute,
  The Nymphs no more their garlands twine:
The Faun hath died upon the hill,
The Naiad by her silver rill.

Time, with his mighty scythe, has passed,
  And mown into the greedy tomb
Empires and creeds; oh, what shall last?
  What triumph o'er the general doom?
We view the winding, classic river,
  It rolls as free, and pure, and bright,
As when the Gaul, with bow and quiver,
  Quailed 'neath the Roman eagle's might;
And flowers blush out, and woods are green;
No lapse, no change, hath Nature seen.

Oh, no—along the earth, the air,
  From mountain-peak, to streamy vale,
Undying youth smiles everywhere,
  Paints the blue sky, and scents the gale.
Then mourn not, man, but snatch a bliss
  From each fair scene that glows around thee;
Let hope the future's bright brow kiss,
  Nor think an evil doom has bound thee!
Bless heaven's decrees, and pluck the flowers,
And give to joy the laughing hours.

Tired day goes down o'er hill and dell,
  Home to her hive the bee is winging;
The lily shuts her velvet bell,
  And his last song the thrush is singing;

Each tiny wave is crisped with gold,
   Bliss clasps all Nature in her arms;
Gleams of Elysium we behold,
   In scene so haunted, full of charms;
And dull is he whose eye would close,
Whose loveless heart no rapture knows

WOMAN'S MODERN ASPIRATIONS.

WHAT want ye, gentle, lovely ones of earth?
   To tread more lofty paths on life's steep hill,
To grasp more power—ah! power of little worth—
   And enter man's domain, and match his skill,
Forgetting that true strength—pure mind, bright eyes,
Heaven gave you first in blissful paradise?

Must that fair hand, soft-shaped with flowers to toy,
   Or lightly move the ivory keys along,
Wield the dissector's knife?   Must lips whose joy
   Should be to whisper love, or warble song,
Strive in the lecture-hall great crowds to draw,
Or wrangle in dull courts of quibbling law?

Woman, why wish, unsexed, to quit the sphere
  Nature through every age proclaimed thine own?
Man hath his fitting tasks, the rough, severe;
  Thy gentle powers still place thee on a throne;
For mental quickness, fancy's fairy play,
And wit's keen flash, thou bear'st the palm away.

In spirit's purity, in thoughts that rise
  Warm, trustful, to the eternal fount of life,
Than man, cold man, thou'rt nearer to the skies;
  Then envy not his toils, his fields of strife;
Descend not from that sweet-aired, lovely height,
O ne'er renounce thy heritage of light!

Think not thy rule too weak, thy range confined;
  Man's heart is thy dominion; frailty grows
A tower of strength through beauty and through mind;
  Where civilization's sunlight brightest glows,
There man to serve thee makes his proudest boast,
There art thou raised the highest, prized the most.

Yet nought may bar thee from the broad, rich field
  Of taste, of learning, poetry, and art;
All these in turn proud triumphs to thee yield,
  So from the graceful ne'er thy steps depart;
Woman plucks flowers along the mountain's side,
Man scales the rocks, and dares the peaks of pride.

What is thy province, fair one, here below?
   To charm in youth and beauty; with bright eyes
To illuminate the twilight shades of woe;
   Where discords reign, to breathe sweet harmonies;
To soothe in sickness, elevate, refine,
And round the brow of care joy's chaplets twine.

To fill with light our dwellings; without thee
   What were each home?   A cold and cheerless spot;
Man fights the fight of life; 'tis thine to be
   The sweet rewarder, crowner of his lot;
The great dispenser of his earthly bliss;
O canst thou more desire, or claim than this?

Repine not at thy mission, pure and high,
   For countless are thy tasks in joy or woe;
Ambition's struggles—there few pleasures lie,
   Thy pleasures from a brighter fountain flow;
Were all the honours thine, man's heart loves best,
Wouldst thou more homage win, or feel more blest?

A river laving banks of varied flowers,
   An ocean heaving turbulent and strong;
A vale by beauty trod, a hill that towers;
   Morn's honeyed breath, a gale that sweeps along;
Such thou and man in life, such either soul,
Your spheres apart, yet one harmonious whole.

MORNING ON RAMSGATE SANDS.

How gay the scene on this smooth, Summer shore,
  Crowded by youth and age, who fly awhile
From smoky cities, life's turmoil and roar,
         And woo dear Nature's smile!

See how the pale cheek glows, as breezes play
  From off the cooling billow! languid eyes
Gaze all refreshed, and steal back health's lost ray
         From sparkling waves and skies!

List to the bright-hair'd children's merry voices,
  As on the sand they build their fragile towers:
Brimming with bliss, each little heart rejoices;
         O happy, reckless hours!

The fond, pleased mother, on that sunny sand,
  Watches their gambols with a quiet pride,
Shading her face, and speaking, smiling bland;
         The father sits aside.

He cons the " news," and oft his straining eye
  Glances far sea-ward, as some stately bark
Moves, like a spirit, 'twixt the wave and sky—
        Wealth's costly-freighted ark.

The maiden leans, love's tale before her set,
  Her jealous hat half screening her sweet face,
Her hair, from ocean's bath, uncurled and wet,
        Hanging in loosened grace.

The enthralling story charms and sways her heart:
  Age of romance, when fancy reigns a queen!
And now she looks around, and seems a part
        Of that bright, lovely scene.

Vague dreams and wishes in her bosom rise;
  Oh, would she were a sea-nymph, or could skim,
Like yon wild bird, the glowing, freshening skies!
        Life real seems so dim.

The boats with white sails gliding to and fro,
  The dipping oar unpractised gallants plying,
The dog that joys in spumy waves to go,
        Seagulls in circles flying.

The slowly-sauntering forms that dot the shore,
  The many-coloured dresses—drowsy calls
Of vendors of rare shells, bright stones, and ore,
      The music's swells and falls.

The air of happiness, the deep serene,
  That seem to wrap each spirit, drawing here
Delight from Nature—such the pleasant scene
      To jaded bosoms dear.

Yes, those bright days by ocean, souls beguiling
  From dull existence, city-toil, and strife,
Are to those hearts a green oasis, smiling
      Mid the parched waste of life.

THE ECHO IN THE VALE.

I HEARD an echo in the vale,
  It floated musically there,
Till the soft-pulsing, fragrant gale
  Seemed love's own melting voice to bear;
    Back from the rocks it fell,
    With silver-softened swell,
And, whispering, died along the air.

What wert thou, Echo? tell me, sweet;
The spirit of some love-lorn maid,
Who would her earthly vows repeat?
Or did some angel charm the shade?
The pure, full anthem ringing,
As all the caves were singing—
A little bird that music made.

Thus oft in life a golden treasure
From source we ne'er expected springs;
Thus oft in life the sweetest pleasure
Will flow from small and trivial things;
Rich echo floated wide,
And all that vale replied,
Charmed by a bird with speckled wings.

THE MEETING OF THE LOVERS.

Those lovers lived where streams ran song,
Far from the city's wildering throng.
We see them at the trysting-place,
Timid as lovers ever are,
At rising of love's early star;
We see his down-bent, pleading face.

The lashes veil her soft brown eyes,
Her bosom checks its tender sighs,
And as in under tones he speaks,
The mounting blushes stain her cheeks,
Red as the new-plucked rose she tears,
In love's dear, absent, winning airs;
And, in that sweet confusion, oft
　She dashes back her falling curls;
While lips, in uttering words most soft,
　Show, through their coral, glistening pearls;
And half she gives him, half withholds,
　The small white hand, and sparkles now
Illume his eyes, as he beholds
　Sweet " yes," upon her smiling brow.

His features glow, and tell how strong
Love's stream that bears his soul along.
Oh, joy most full—oh, dream most sweet,
　That trembling hearts on earth can bless,
Where all dear thoughts, warm feelings meet—
　Accepted love's first happiness !—
On wood, and stream, and hamlet, lie
　The soft rich tints of dying day;
The cattle low as eve draws nigh,
The lark drops music from the sky,
　The mavis answering far away;

The wild flowers shut their sleepy bells,
Bees, honey-laden, seek their cells,
While Peace, like some white angel, flies
Between the earth and fading skies,
Hushing the world as stars unclose,
Bringing to mortals kind repose.—
They grow more calm 'mid that serene,
  Their hearts with bliss are brimming o'er,
And love throws beauty on the scene,
  That ne'er such beauty owned before.

THE PRESENT HOUR.

THE present hour—small fragment, speck of time!
What human joy, what agony, what crime,
It doth condense!—thought terrible, sublime!

This hour to us how brief! yet, while 'tis flying,
Earthquakes may shake far lands, towns ruins lying;
Thousands to life are springing, thousands dying.

What multitudes this moment feast and drink,
Or lightly tread the dance, nor pause to think!
What multitudes shed tears, or, starving, sink!

How many in luxurious rooms recline
On couches soft, while lamps above them shine,
Listening to love's sweet voice, and airs divine!

How many the same instant on the wave.
Are tost by storms! they shriek, but none can save,
And, shrieking, sink in ocean's greedy grave.

What virtuous spirits sorrow, wrong'd, oppress'd!
What hearts, long parted, meet, supremely blest!
What bitter, sad farewells wring many a breast!

E'en as these pulses beat, how many a sigh
Of pity melts around! how many an eye
Is raised in meek devotion to the sky!

E'en as these pulses beat, the murderer steals
On his hushed way—his deadly thought conceals—
He crouches, springs, the stroke of horror deals!

Ring out, this hour, a thousand marriage-bells,
Joy's revelry for thousand christenings swells,
Toll mournfully a thousand funeral knells.

What countless lovers whisper, 'neath the shade,
Eternal truth—alas ! for many a maid !
Unnumbered hearts are breaking, love-betrayed !

What floods and fires are raging, as we lean
In calmness here ! while, startling heaven's serene,
War's thunder now may burst on many a scene !

O'er desert moors what houseless wretches wend !
From beds of anguish what sad groans ascend !
What mothers o'er their dying offspring bend !

All this, all this, while a few moments fly ;
Moments so full of fate, to heaven that cry,
Charged with all passions—bliss and misery !

We talk, feast, laugh, enjoy the sun's glad light,
But little dream what scenes, the dark, the bright,
Are crowded in one hour's eventful flight.

THE BURIAL OF A YOUNG OFFICER
AT SEA.

Sickening, he died, far on the Tropic ocean,
  Where skies seem flame,
His last word, as he quivered with emotion,
  His mother's name.

The sun was dropping westward, slowly, slowly :
  Winds lulled away ;
Each wave caught heaven's rich splendour; something
    holy
  On nature lay.

The nautilus his painted shell was guiding,
  Dolphins gleamed past ;
The vessel, on the burnished billow riding,
  Long shadows cast.

We brought him upon deck, the awning under,
   Bravery now low,
No more to hear the cannon's rolling thunder
   Or front the foe.

We looked again upon his face, and, stooping,
   Kissed his young brow,
Then placed him in his shroud, the colours drooping,
   All silent now.

There lay he ready—he late mirth and gladness—
   For his sea-grave;
And many a heart, ne'er touched before by sadness,
   A deep sigh gave.

We stood with folded hands and heads uncovered,
   Before the dead;
The albatross above the vessel hovered,
   As the priest read.

Oh! didst thou hear those solemn words, thou ocean,
   Making low moan?
Thou azure sepulchre, with murmuring motion,
   Asking thine own!

The clay to thy cold keeping must be given,
  The soul above;
But one had died to save him—pity, Heaven,
  That heart of love!

How would she weep when told the mournful story!
  Her darling brave,
Not slain in fight, and giv'n a wreath of glory,
  But this sad grave.

We lowered him slowly, gently to the billow;
  We gazed once more;
Sleep, much-loved comrade, sleep on thy cold pillow!
  One splash—'twas o'er.

Thus to the depths mysterious we committed
  The mother's pride;
The waves above him swept, the sea-bird flitted,
  And low winds sighed.

On ocean's verge the broad, flushed sun was resting,
  Twilight brought balm,
Beauty, solemnity, the scene investing
  With holiest calm.

There let him slumber far from gentle weepers,
  In coral caves,
Till the last trumpet calls the long, long sleepers
  From their sea-graves.

THE BEAUTIFUL LADY.

The beautiful lady has raven hair,
  Or auburn softly-gleaming ;
Her forehead is ample, smooth, and fair,
  Her eyes are large and beaming ;
Blue as we paint the angel's eyes,
  Or dark, their fire repressing ;
Her cheek has the warmth of Summer skies,
  Dimples soul's gladness expressing.

The beautiful lady's oval face
  By its sweetness hearts will win ;
Like the moon, it borrows its brightness and grace
  From a sun, the spirit within ;
Yes, mind o'er the sparkling features will play,
  And worth write its letters of gold ;
Without them she looks but lovely clay,
  A model in marble cold.

The beautiful lady is tall and slight,
    But graceful in every motion;
And her walk is like the sailing light
    Of a ship on a glassy ocean;
But a beauty in form less tall is shrined,
    With loving eyes witching us still,
With a lightsome step, and a cheerful mind,
    All smiles like a sunshiny rill.

The beautiful lady can pensive be,
    And thought on her brow will sit;
But oft'ner she tosses her head in glee,
    And wins by her laughter and wit:
Oh, that laughter which doth from a glad heart ring,
    Showing pearly teeth red lips through,
Like the bird's happy song in opening Spring,
    Enchants while it gladdens us too.

The beautiful lady is loved by all,
    For beauty were valueless here,
Did its beams uncharmingly, coldly fall,
    Its smiles nor treasured nor dear:
No sullenness ever her face will shade,
    Good humour still sparkling there,
As a lovely flower more lovely is made
    By the sun on a morning fair.

The beautiful lady will never forget
   Her gentleness, gracious to all ;
The virtues, like roses around her set,
   Shedding sweets that never can pall :
No scorn on her brow, she cannot be proud
   To her peers, to the needy or low ;
And still, like a star that gilds a dark cloud,
   Her presence sheds brightness on woe.

THE OLD CHURCH PORCH.

THE old church porch—encircling ivy seems,
Like sanctity, to shut out worldly dreams,
While from the west eve's slanting glory streams.

Each patch of moss, the arch so worn and grey,
Entered by generations past away,
The rude stone bench—all catch the mellow ray.

The dial, through the ages, fixed on high,
Tells thoughtful gazers how poor moments fly,
Time's finger pointing to eternity.

The dead sleep near unheeding sun or shower,
The last bee hums around the churchyard flower,
The clamorous daw slow seeks the mouldering tower.

How many passed this porch in ancient day,
Called by the bell from moorlands far away,
Good, simple hearts, to worship God and pray!

I see, borne fondly in, the infant child,
I see the rough, pleased father, mother mild,
Offering that babe a Christian undefiled.

Now the once infant enters with his bride,
Smiling in love, and flushed in manhood's pride,
And soon the marriage-bells peal far and wide.

Hush! there is wailing! from each cottage-door,
Sedate and sad, the humble inmates pour,
To lay tired age where mortals toil no more.

They bear him through the porch; the rustic weeps;
Infant and bridegroom, now the patriarch sleeps,
And the sad bell o'er hill and valley sweeps.

Thus through the porch hath time's calm, slow career
Sent generations, once beloved and dear;
Now o'er their dust few living drop a tear.

But still the ivy trails its solemn green,
The red-rimmed daisy at the porch is seen,
And, friend of death, the yew-tree spreads serene.

And still mild evening shoots its slanting ray,
Warming the moss, the walls so old and gray,
As if an angel bent to earth its way:

And smiled on this old porch, and kissed the flowers;
And hark! a linnet trills soft music-showers,
Adding a charm to evening's sainted hours.

Oh, ancient porch! we dream small histories here,
Witness of many a smile and silent tear,
Each mouldered stone to thoughtful memory dear.

REST.

The sun hath quickened earth with burning eye,
   Expanding flowers and brightening seas and rills,
And now, his journey finished in the sky,
   He goes to sleep behind the curtained hills;
Trees droop their leaves, each bird hath sought its nest,
        Vales, mountains, call for rest.

Summer hath flushed the plains with warmth and bloom,
  And tasked the ground's fertility and strength;
Autumn hath reaped her stores; the last perfume
  Dies in the vale, and winter comes at length;
Nature lies down with snow-wreaths on her breast,
      And asks recruiting rest.

The child is chasing butterflies, and laughs,
  And pants across the meads, with cheeks a-glow;
The sweetest wine of life its spirit quaffs,
  Mocking, dear reckless thing, at care and woe;
And yet the happy one, soon worn, oppressed,
      Drops into smiling rest.

The rustic strains his sinews at the plough,
  Content to toil, not think, the live-long day;
He hears the village-clock, and wipes his brow,
  And plods, with cheerful smile, his homeward way:
Amidst his babes, what makes his heart so blest?
      'Tis labour's guerdon, rest.

The wealthy city merchant, passing life
  In ceaseless tumult, planning, heaping gold,
Awaits the time when, ended toil and strife,
  His wearied eyes shall some calm scene behold,
Some spot remote, where his long harassed breast
      Shall taste the sweets of rest.

When age makes white the head, and sears the heart,
  And joy's drained cup hath little more to yield,
And we are called with those we love to part,
  The last poor fainting gleaners in life's field,
What hope remains to soothe the mourner's breast?
        The hope of heaven's bright rest.

THE CONVALESCENT.

'Twas a calm morn in Spring; the sun, bright glancing,
  Shot life to earth;
The air was soft, and little rills ran dancing
  In light and mirth.

She wandered forth, though feeble still, and whiteness
  Her cheek o'erspread;
But oh, once more dear health's long absent brightness
  Her soft eyes shed.

Slowly she trod the garden walks; keen pleasure
  Her senses thrilled;
Each flower seemed grown more lovely—a rich treasure
  Which beauty filled.

The lark, high up, his joy to morning telling,
   On winnowing wing,
Was like her heart, where happiness was swelling,
   And yearned to sing.

After long drooping in a close, dull room,
   With feeble breath,
Racked by keen pain, and curtain'd in still gloom,
   Expecting death :

How blest, delightful, down the lane to ramble,
   And pluck the May !
There was a beauty e'en in fern and bramble,
   Veiled till that day.

Ne'er did the village to the squire's young daughter
   So bright appear ;
The ragged children, playing by the water,
   Seemed fair and dear.

The drowsy bells' low chimings, from the tower,
   Like voices, stole ;
More sweet, more touching, than in health's gay hour,
   They soothed her soul.

She reached the upland ; far beneath were flowing
　　Waves with low roar ;
Never so blue as now, so brightly glowing,
　　They kissed the shore.

Oh, that loved sea ! to view again its splendour,
　　And hear its voice,
Bade soul deep thanks to her Creator render,
　　And heart rejoice.

She raised her eyes to heaven—soft blue to blue—
　　And, lowly kneeling,
To tears she yielded, while thought upward flew,
　　On wings of feeling.

DREAMING OF PARADISE.

Dreaming, dreaming through the noon-day hours,
　　Thinking where that far, blissful region lies,
Region of living streams and fadeless flowers—
　　Dreaming of paradise ;

Where they who lately trod
This weary, darkened sod,
In vales of beauty stray,
Dashing all tears away.

Dreaming, dreaming at the sunset time,
   Watching the glories of the western skies,
That burn with opal gates, and towers sublime—
   Dreaming of paradise;
Thinking if that rich road
Leads to the blest abode—
Those ruby walls the bound
Of Heaven's wide dazzling ground.

Dreaming, dreaming, gazing through the night,
   While swiftly upwards trembling fancy flies,
Hailing the stars as finger-posts of light,
   Pointing to paradise:
Asking if Hope may view
Heaven's seats in that deep blue,
Where harp, beyond the dim,
The fire-soul'd seraphim.

Dreaming, dreaming, pondering on the hours
   When Eden bloomed on earth, and angel-eyes
Smiled on the dwellers of those radiant bowers—
   Mourning for paradise;

There man first breathed ; at last,
When mortal ills are past,
Again he shall be blest
With bowers of endless rest.

Dreaming, dreaming, fancying what may be
  The employment of the happy in the skies ;
Will they hive knowledge through eternity,
  Or love in paradise ?
View glories near and far,
Journey from star to star,
Or join the seraph-throng,
Filling Heaven's halls with song ?

Dreaming, dreaming, thinking how the soul,
  Freed from Earth's cumbering chains, will upward rise ;
How it will pass the glory-clouds that roll,
  Infolding paradise ;
Of meetings there ; delight
That naught will dim or blight ;
No grave, no sighs, no tears,
Through blest eternal years.

FAR AT SEA.

Far away upon the sea,
  On the deck my watch I keep;
Ocean, like eternity,
  Doth around me grandly sweep;
Night is striving to be dark,
  But the throbbing stars, bright shining,
Make each broken wave a spark,
  And our sails with pearls are lining;
Softly breezes die and swell,
Like strange murmurs in the shell.

Far away upon the sea,
  Pacing slowly, thinking, dreaming,
Turn my thoughts, loved home, to thee,
  Sun upon fond memory beaming.
What a waste of water lies
  'Twixt me and my native bowers!
O'er its paths I waft my sighs,
  Musing on dear vanished hours;
Slow I sail, yet not in gladness,
Every league but deepens sadness.

Far away upon the sea,
　　Hastening south, but looking north;
All the world seems flood to me,
　　And my thoughts, like doves, go forth:
Yes, they fly, and now alight
　　On old elm-trees in a valley;
There I see—dear, touching sight—
　　House, moss'd pond, and garden alley,
And the clock-tower, with its bell,
And the dog I loved so well.

Far away upon the sea—
　　Hush! it is not fancy all;
O'er the waves' immensity
　　Murmurs float, and rise, and fall;
'Tis the village bells I hear,
　　Charming once our Evening skies,
Sounds to happy childhood dear,
　　Ringing as from paradise:
Oh, that music o'er the deep!
Let me listen—let me weep.

Far away upon the sea—
　　Hush! it is not fancy all;
O'er the waves' immensity
　　Silvery voices seem to call:

'Tis my Sister's, as her tresses
  Float, bright-shining, in the sun;
'Tis my Mother's, as she blesses,
  Blesses me, her wandering son;
Oh, those voices o'er the deep!
Let me listen—let me weep.

THE BURNING EMIGRANT SHIP.

(FOR RECITATION.)

BRAVELY she walks the ocean,
  With smooth and stately motion,
Gliding in beauty tow'rd the glowing West;
  The yellow beams are burning
  On wide-spread sails, and turning
To glossy gold each little billow's breast:
  Gaily the deck they throng,
  Some chase the hour with song;
On western shores they seek another home;
  Lovers on maidens glance,
  And now in groups they dance,
While music makes more smooth the shining foam.

Go down, thou sleepy sun, with burnished brow !
    Drop, drop the waters o'er !
Glad eyes that greet thy beams of splendour now,
    May view those beams no more.
    See that thin smoke—a tiny cloud,
    Near where young maids are laughing loud;
    'Tis nothing, nothing—pipe the lay,
    And merry dancers, dance away !
    Forth from the cabin now it curls
    In darker whiffs, and wider whirls !
    Then low is heard a crackling sound;
    With sudden glare, and eager bound,
    Up springs a column, redder, higher—
    O cease your songs—'tis fire ! 'tis fire !

    The seamen to and fro are rushing,
    And torrents o'er the decks are gushing :
" Put out the fire ! more water, more !"
    Still goes the cry,
    But red on high
Ascend the flames with hiss and roar.
    The emigrants are white,
    And shivering with affright;
    Their instruments are mute,
    The viol, horn, and flute,
    Cast wildly on the deck,
    Where all is maddening wreck :

" Put out the fire ! more water, more !"
        Still goes the cry,
        But red on high
Leap up the flames with fiercer roar.

Around the masts, like snakes, those flames are curling ;
        The sails are all a-blaze,
Like ensigns, dyed with blood, to gales unfurling ;
        Demons, well pleased, might gaze.
Up the tarr'd ropes the fire's dread fury flies,
        Quick messengers of fear,
To bear the tale of horror to the skies—
        Hark ! what appals the ear ?
'Tis strong men's shouts that die along the wave,
The shrieks of women praying God to save ;
Will no good angel come to snatch from doom ?
Or must that ship go down, a fiery tomb ?

The boats are launched ; some rush, some leap ;
        ˙A tithe of that wild throng,
        Hurrying the decks along,
Would whelm those boats beneath the deep :
Burdened they heel, but on the saved they bear ;
        Hearts bleed to leave behind
        Dear friends a grave to find
In that hot furnace of despair.

P

Alas ! for the remaining crowd !
Hark to their wailings loud !
Poor wretches, near the bow,
Like sheep, they gather now,
As if by grouping they could fly
Their doom of fear and agony.
And so that ship on fire
Burns like a funeral pyre ;
She drifts along the shimmering, blood-red waves,
The heaving, glossy, fire-reflecting waves,
Like burnished tomb-stones for their coming graves.

Piteous, heart-rending sight ! some mutely there
Stand shivering, paralysed, in white despair ;
And some, heroic spirits, front grim death,
With hands firm-clenched, raised brow, and bated breath ;
While others on the heated deck are kneeling,
Praying to God, their eyes calm light revealing :
A mother here strains wildly to her breast
The unconscious infant, nestling into rest,
Casts off the sparks that 'round in showers are thrown,
And in its danger half forgets her own.
Husbands are clasping wives, and lovers cling
Madly unto each other, as they wring
An anguished rapture from that last embrace,
Kissing each other's hair, and eyes, and face,

Viewing the raging fire, the pitiless main,
And weeping floods of tears, how vain! how vain!

The emigrants, hemmed, scorching now,
Behold the flames approach the bow;
They come, creep, creep,
Devouring as they sweep;
Cross fire-jets fiercely flashing,
Prone fall the masts, loud crashing;
Creep, creep—the burnt yards hiss,
Hot seems the very abyss;
Through flames the ship is reeling,
Smoke her black hull concealing;
With mirrored fire each wave is crowned,
Fire here, fire there, fire all around.

A ship! a ship!—upon the ocean's brim
It whitens, grows—it flashes through the dim:
A ship! a ship! she's steaming o'er the wave,
Swift as morn's sea-bird darting from her cave.
She comes! all eyes are tow'rd that vision cast,
Their shrieks of rapture swelling down the blast.
She comes! the white foam feathering at her bow,
Her colours streaming high, to hail them now.
Oh, will the flames delay?   Heaven, hear their prayer!
They hang 'twixt life and death, 'twixt hope, despair.

Dash on, thou gallant ship! urge, urge thy way!
Defraud the flames, and snatch from death its prey.
The emigrants, with straining eyes, look out,
And toss their arms, their souls in each wild shout.
She comes with rushing bow, and whirring wheel,
And her good, urgent mission seems to feel.
She nears the bark; the wide-spread fire she'll brave;
Her boats are lower'd, and dashing on to save:
The emigrants fast crowd them, maiden fair,
Small child, and feeble age, the strong man's care;
And still boats haste away, approach again,
Saving, like angels, those joy-maddened men.
Now all in safety placed, they watch afar
The burning ship, like some huge fiery star.
She labours, heels, ere plunging to her grave,
A cone of flame, a furnace on the wave.
Great fish, attracted, to the surface sweep,
Behold the blaze, and, startled, dive more deep;
While sea-birds, wheeling near, fly off in fright,
With piercing screams at that strange, dreadful light.
Another heel—thick sparks—the heavens a-glow,
One boiling hiss—she sinks in gulfs below.
Oh, how the saved ones bless their saviours now,
Shake hands, embrace, joy brightening every brow;
Till pent-up feelings burst in one wild cry,
And long, long shouts of rapture mount the sky.

THE LILY OF EDEN.

Sweet virgin lily, charming Spring's gay hours!
How old thy race! thine ancestors, bright flowers,
Decking before the flood the vales and bowers.

Ages have altered not thy soft, pale cheek,
Thy drooping forehead, silky, fair, and meek,
Thy form of elegance, though slim and weak.

Did Eve esteem one flower above the rest
Blooming in Eden?   Lily, whitely drest,
Sure it was thou—thee, thee, she loved the best.

O lily—it is no fantastic dream—
She viewed thee mirrored in Euphrates' stream,
Thy lithe stem turned to gold in evening's beam.

Thy snowy bell she hung o'er with pleased eye,
Admired those petals, drank thine odorous sigh,
Then in her bosom bade thy beauty lie.

And since Eve loved thee for thy spotless white,
Flower! thou hast been, in each young maiden's sight,
A type of purity, and virtue bright.

Nature designed thee, with thy drooping eye,
Thy timid head, ne'er proudly tossed on high,
To image grace, and preach of modesty.

As now the happy bee around thee wings,
And, dallying near, the mated throstle sings,
And thy sweet censer zephyr gently swings:

I hail thee fairy-queen among the flowers,
Now brightening in the sun, now soft in showers,
The loveliest relic of lost Eden's bowers.

O that my soul were stainless, pure as thou,
Unmarr'd by time, no shadow on thy brow!
Eve bless'd thee once, then let us love thee now.

BEAUTIFUL THINGS.

———

THE world is full of beauty, though at times
   'Tis darkened by calamity and ill;
And did not man spread misery by his crimes,
   'Twould be a smiling, blessëd Eden still :·
Visions before me pass ; below, above,
I see but things of beauty, proofs of love.

O sunset sky ! where day drinks ruby wine,
   Those opal clouds the goblets brimming o'er ;
Rich sky, where angels glowing tissues twine,
   To robe new comers on heaven's pearly shore ;
Gold bars, the steps that up to glory rise ;
Red vistas stretching into paradise.

O stars, the jewels on night's dusky robe !
   The altar-fires to God, extinguished never'!
Doth not a glory crown each beauteous globe,
   Singing and shining on for ever, ever ?
Each star a favoured land, that may not know
The storms which shake us here, nor crime, nor woe.

Flowers of the wild—the smallest bloom that chides
　The amorous winds, by Nature's handmaid drest,
Offers a wonder, and, sweet coy one, hides
　A world of beauty in its folded breast;
Flowers cheering, lighting up the grateful sod,
First dropped on earth, embodied smiles of God.

Clear, glassy fountain, from soft moss up-bubbling,
　Toying with pebbles, singing through the reeds,
No taint its mountain-born, cool crystal troubling,
　Pure through its depths as mercy's holy deeds:
River, broad river, swiftly rolled along,
Mirror of clouds, a full-voiced, joyous song.

The rustling wood, when Autumn's many dyes
　Burn on the twinkling leaves, or richly throw
A blood-red glory rivalling sunset skies;
　The fainting splendour of the aërial bow,
Gorgeously graceful, beautifully still,
With glowing feet on either tinted hill.

I stand upon the shore, and watch the play
　Of billows heaving in their glassy glory,
Then breaking on the shells in diamond spray,
　Weird music echoing soft from caverns hoary:
Oh, what a beauty lies on ocean's plains,
The seagull's Eden, grandeur's wide domains!

The world is full of beauty; living things
  Enchant us too with loveliness; we see
Its happy charm in birds with painted wings,
  And graceful animals, the wild, the free;
But most it clothes the human form, which stands
God's shining image, moulded by His hands.

The world is full of beauty; 'tis ideal
  The gloom which pining discontent beholds;
Sunshine, fair form, heaven's smiles, adorn the real;
  Let us enjoy what bounteous earth unfolds,
And thank kind Nature that around us glow
These lovely things to cheer our path below.

PROGRESS.

Progress! progress! all things cry;
  Progress, Nature's golden rule;
Nothing tarries 'neath the sky;
  Learn in Nature's wondrous school:

Earth from chaos sprang sublime,
  Broad-armed oaks from acorns grow;
Insects, labouring, build in time
  Mighty islands from below:
Press we on thro' good and ill,
Progress be our watchword still!

Rough may be the mountain-road
  Leading to the heights of Mind;
Climb, and reach Truth's bright abode,
  Dull the souls that grope behind.
Science, learning, yield their prize,
  Faint not in the noble chase,
He who aims not to be wise,
  Sinks unworthy of his race:
He who fights shall vanquish ill;
Progress be our watchword still!

Broad the tract that lies before us,
  Never mourn the days of old,
Sighs will not tombed years restore us,
  Past is iron—future gold!
Savage! learn till civilised;
  Slave! your fetters shake till free;
Hearts that struggle, souls despised!
  Work your own high destiny:

All things yield to steadfast will,
Progress be our watchword still!

Onward! Orient nations know
  Nothing of that magic word;
'Tis the trump that giants blow,
  'Tis the spirit's conquering sword!
'Tis the electric, mystic fire
  Which should flash around the earth,
Making every heart a wire—
  'Tis a word of heavenly birth:
Onward! at the sound we thrill;
Progress be our watchword still.

THE RAY OF LIGHT.

THE ray, the ruddy ray of morn!
  It shoots from eastern hills,
With glory crowns the old church-tower;
  It plays on moss-lipped rills,
And with a warm, soft, amber light,
  Each dewy flower-cup fills.

The ray, the blithesome ray of morn !
  Joy to the bee 'tis bringing ;
It wakes the spotted butterfly,
  A living pansy winging ;
It pierces the brown gloom of woods,
  And sets the birds a-singing.

The ray, the beauteous ray of morn !
  It paints the ruin old,
Cheats the sad ivy into smiles,
  And where pale Death doth fold
His silent flock, it gilds the tombs,
  Gilds them with softest gold.

The ray, the healthful ray of morn !
  It calls the lusty boor,
And sends him forth to wield the scythe,
  Or plough the daisied moor,
And bids his fresh-cheeked daughter milk
  The red cow at the door.

The ray, the bold, free ray of morn !
  It steals, and slyly creeps
Through pane, and half-drawn curtain white,
  Where high-born beauty sleeps,
And, kissing brow, and loose black curls,
  Richness in richness steeps.

The ray, the merry ray of morn !
  Calmly a babe reposes;
Light wakes it, like a flow'ret, up,
  Its glad, blue eye uncloses;
To catch that beam, arms open wide,
  While glow the cheek's bright roses.

The ray, the cheering ray of morn !
  Through bars it gently steals,
Where weeps the captive in his cell;
  Light to his heart appeals;
It tells him of the far, free hills,
  And joy awhile he feels.

The ray, the placid ray of morn !
  It trembles down the skies,
And makes the room more hallowed, calm,
  Where a maid dying lies;
To greet that last beam—ah ! the last,
  She feebly opes her eyes.

The ray, the holy ray of morn !
  All gently as a dove,
It speeds, a messenger from God,
  And tells her of His love,
That angels come, on shining wings,
  To bear her soul above,

THE ORIENTAL BEAUTY.

DARK as starless, wintry night,
  Fall her glossy ebon curls,
Loosely bound with circlet bright,
  Reaching to her zone of pearls.

Smooth as veinless Parian stone,
  Wrought to life by Attic skill,
Mellowing sunbeams on it thrown,
  Shines that brow, serene and still.

Warm as hues to Nature given,
  When the sun in ocean dips—
Hues that burn on blushing heaven—
  Glow her cheeks and smiling lips.

Black and large as the gazelle's,
  Soft as April's showery skies,
Home where Orient passion dwells,
  Beam her sleepy, oval eyes.

Supple as the streamlet's willow,
  All too weak to front the storm,
Pressing the rich silken pillow,
  Slothful leans her graceful form.

Nursed in luxury, taught to think
  Little of the worth of mind,
Caring not to rise or sink,
  To her narrow sphere resigned;

See her wreathing emblem-flowers,
  Sporting with her prison'd dove,
While her slave, to charm the hours,
  Sings from Hafiz lays of love.

Oh, let western maidens climb
  Hard Improvement's toilsome steep,
Soar on fancy's wing sublime,
  And thy harvest, Learning, reap:

Give her all the senses ask—
    Odours, jewels, gaudy dress—
She'll resign each mental task,
    Lapp'd in downy idleness.

Such is beauty in those climes
    Where a warmer summer laughs,
And the spirit, through all times,
    Luxury's sweetest poison quaffs.

Such that beauty, like a dream
    Each voluptuous, aimless day,
Idling in the rich hareem,
    Careless smiling life away.

THE DYING FLOWER-GIRL.

O BRING me flowers! I would once more
    Gaze on their long-loved, sunny bloom,
Kiss their bright leaves ere life be o'er,
    And die upon their rich perfume;
Man shapes his gems, God made the flowers,
Wafted to earth from heaven's own bowers.

O give me flowers! my childhood's day
   Passed 'mid their sweets, but ne'er again
My hand shall pluck them, decking gay
   The lane, the wood, or mossy glen,
No more shall bear the fragrant spoil,
Death ending now my happy toil.

O give me flowers! their rich, soft dyes
   Of innocence and virtue speak;
Methinks the angels in yon skies
   Are, like earth's flow'rets, pure and meek;
Bright things, they sure might bloom above,
Symbols of peace and holy love.

O give me flowers! as I depart
   My lips would drink their honeyed breath,
Their odours, while they glad my heart,
   Will chase the faintness e'en of death:
Place them before my closing eye,
I'll bless them, think of God, and die.

I hold them now, sweet, precious things,
   Dear lowly glories of the field;
As musing memory backward wings,
   These flowers a farewell rapture yield;
They speak to me of blissful years,
Unmark'd by pain, undimmed by tears.

The love I've read of, burning strong
  In woman's breast, through youth's warm hours;
The love that bards have given to song,
  I've lavished on those idol-flowers;
The passion, like a deepening stream,
Strengthens with life's fast-closing dream.

And when this heart shall cease to beat,
  Let flowers beside me breathe perfume;
O let me take them, fresh and sweet,
  Types of life's morning, to the tomb;
And on the turf, in after hours,
Spring up! spring up! dear worshipp'd flowers.

PAST AND FUTURE.

WHAT is gone time?—a bodiless dream, a thought,
  Our hopes, our wishes, it will claim no more;
The future lures us, with strong magic fraught,
  The soul still looks before.

What is gone time ?—a flash of lightning spent,
    And quenched within the ocean deep and drear,
But lingering thunders still to earth are sent—
    So men's deeds echo here.

What is gone time ?—a wind that did caress
    Our brows like balm—that summer odours bore,
Now swept away to some far wilderness,
    To soothe our sense no more.

What is gone time ?—the gorgeous crimson light
    That Artist-Eve spread o'er the sunset sky ;
'Tis fled we know not where, as falls the night,
    Leaving us but to sigh.

What is the future ?—a great book, whose leaves,
    . Clasped by the fates, are opened but by God ;
A sea's deep bottom ; the near surface heaves ;
    That bottom never trod.

O past ! O future ! while we live between
    The two eternities, let grief be given
For wasted years ; we'll sail the present scene,
    Anchoring our hopes in heaven.

A CORNISH VILLAGE.

The sun just peeps above the ferny hills,
  Blushing and bashful as a hind in love,
Shooting his rays oblique on misty rills;
  But, soon more bold, he springs the woods above,
And gazes with broad face and eyes of mirth,
Upon his bride—the peaceful, modest earth.

The village clock strikes six; more bright the skies;
  And now the humble tenants are astir;
Thin smoke-wreaths o'er each cottage bluely rise,
  Where housewives kindle fires of peat or fir,
Sprinkle o'er rude stone floors the yellow sand,
And spread the frugal meal with active hand.

Now Labour carries out God's first intent,
  That each in busy tasks a part should bear;
The strong-necked oxen to the plough are bent,
  The rustic whistles o'er the shining share;
The mower whets his scythe upon the hill,
And clatter, clatter, works the busy mill.

But see, who comes from yon low cottage-door,
  In spreading hat, with sun-tanned arms all bare?
Light as her heart, her foot the grass trips o'er;
  She looks to eyes of peasants passing fair;
Her form is softly rounded, cheeks are roses,
And quiet archness on her lip reposes.

She treads the meadow, and the cattle know her,
  The calf frisks round her with its sides of silk;
Love e'en the timid lambs, by bleating, show her;
  Hark! in the shining pail the splashing milk:
The kingcups, looking on her, seem to smile,
The happy maid blithe singing all the while.

The thresher, in the neighbouring barn, throws down
  The ringing flail; he stands beside her now;
Rustic coquette, she turns from him, a frown
  Striving to darken her young, pretty brow:
And then she blushes, while she lets him bear
Her milk-pail home, and thanks him laughing there.

The sun is near mid heaven; luxurious heat
  Faints o'er the landscape; flowers their heads bend low;
The birds, close-bower'd, have ceased their descant sweet;
  Delicious 'tis to hear the cool stream flow,
Faint gurgling, tuning through the trembling reeds,
While the fish darts, the green-necked mallard feeds.

The lazy cart-wheels turn more slowly round,
  And where the village sage his school doth keep,
You hear a buzzing and uncertain sound,
  From master tired, and urchins half asleep;
The old dog panting in the door-way sits,
The dame her needle plies, and nods by fits.

But in the hay-field all is busy life;
  They toss, and toss the flakes of clover sweet;
Richly it smells, with Nature's odours rife,
  Refreshing sense beneath the withering heat!
Bared are men's arms, tucked short the maidens' dresses,
Kerchiefs untied, while loosely fall their tresses.

They toss the hay, and oft the jocund hind
  Indulges some bold jest, and laughter rings
Lightly from rosy lips, and where they find
  Hay heaped more high, the daring peasant springs—
The season's privilege—love's harmless bliss—
Making the hay more sweet with many a kiss.

Go down, go down, thou hot-faced Summer sun!
  Let freshness bless again the thirsty earth;
Come out, ye hiding birds, from coverts dun,
  And pipe your evening songs of joy and mirth!
Lift your bowed heads, ye flowers! by brake and pool,
And drink the nectarous dew, enjoy the cool.

Released from toil, the village folk are meeting;
  Some saunter slowly, some on benches lean,
Wives telling tales, old men the old men greeting,
  While noisy children gambol on the green:
The late quick mill-wheel flashes round no more,
The flail is silent on the threshing-floor.

Now down the elm-walk happy lovers rove,
  Plighting their vows; but nought the lusty hind
Regards love's star pale rising o'er the grove;
  Gentle romance ne'er warmed his stolid mind;
He tells his honest tale in plainest style,
And she can blush acceptance, sigh, and smile.

Thus in that Cornish village life goes round,
  Toil and repose—the hills, the vales, their home;
Their simple joys to narrowest circle bound,
  Here were they born, nor ask their hearts to roam;
Heroes may fight, or thrones in dust be hurled,
Calm pass their years—this, this their little world.

THE LOVELIEST THING ON EARTH.

WHAT is the loveliest thing upon earth?
  The curious, inquiring spirit cries;
Or is there nothing of passing worth,
  Since God closed the gates of Paradise?

Is it the sea, when the wearied deep
  Lies hushed in repose, the shore its white pillow,
And the stars, angel-eyes, are watching its sleep,
  And the moon sees her face in the glass of each billow?

Or is it a stately ship on that ocean,
  With snowy sails spread, just leaving the shore,
Now stooping, now gliding with dignified motion,
  Like a sea-goddess walking the crystalline floor

Is it the river that now dashes proudly,
   Now kisses sweet islets, and sparkles along?
Is it the vale when morn, laughing loudly,
   Warms it with beams, and fills it with song?

Is it the rainbow that stands in the skies,
   A ladder with opal rounds, shafts rich-impearled,
Where angels descend, with love-beaming eyes,
   And gorgeous wings shining, to visit our world?

Is it the sunset when cherubim seem,
   With fingers of fire, a curtain to raise,
And mortals a moment, in privileged dream,
   On heaven's bright palaces ravished may gaze?

Tell me, O tell me the loveliest thing
   Delighting our minds, while charming our eyes!
'Tis nothing that glorious Nature can bring,
   But the sweet shrine of something akin to the skies.

'Tis the being who gave to Eden's blest bowers
   A warmth and a charm till her birth all unknown;
Her smiles added smiles to the beautiful flowers,
   And the angels mistook her for one of their own.

Now the cot and the palace her presence makes bright,
  Her strength in her lovely weakness doth lie;
She walks all unconscious of beauty and light,
  As the star that knows nought of its splendour on high.

'Tis woman, 'tis woman, her calm, witching face
  Illumined by feeling, and mirroring worth,
Her brow thought's throne, and her form breathing
    grace—
  Oh, this is the loveliest thing upon earth.

SPIRITS EVERYWHERE.

On soft gales that morn is bringing,
  Over wood, and hill, and lea,
Spirits may be ever winging,
  Though our eyes no form can see;
They may hear the blithe birds singing,
  Mark gay flower, and waving tree,
Revel in the fountain springing,
  Like its waters bright and free;

Hanging on the odorous air,
Glorying in the pure and fair,
Spirits, spirits, everywhere.

When the moon is whitely shining
    On the level ocean-floor,
Stars their woof of beam-threads twining,
    Thick they crowd the glimmering shore.
They love ocean's soft repining,
    Music, too, its louder roar;
On the foam their shades reclining,
  · Ocean's ruler they adore,
Looking up through silvery air,
Loving the sublime and fair,
Spirits, spirits, everywhere.

All the globes with life are teeming;
    Nought is empty, nought is vain;
Peopling ether is not dreaming,
    Space, wide space the soul's domain:
Down they glide, and, round us beaming,
    Share our joy, lament our pain,
Good hearts more than proud esteeming,
    Breathing heaven on vale and plain;
Messages to earth they bear,
Making human souls their care,
Spirits, spirits, everywhere.

THE GUARDIAN ANGEL AND CHILD.

———

Guardian angels, breathing love,
　　Issue ever from heaven's portals,
Sent by Him who rules above,
　　Though unseen by dim-eyed mortals.

One of those bright creatures now
　　Glided from the seats Elysian,
With a glory round her brow,
　　Shining like a golden vision.

To our earth she shaped her flight,
　　Leaving in her path of fleetness
A long train of silvery light,
　　Singing thus with heavenly sweetness.

Swiftly, swiftly, down the skies,
   I will haste at pity's calling,
Where the light from evening's eyes
   On yon lovely isle is falling.

Sweetly, sweetly, the perfume
   Floateth up from summer roses;
Round the humble cot they bloom,
   Where the mortal child reposes.

Gently, gently, wings I'll fold
   O'er the infant-cherub sleeping—
Curtains of soft downy gold,
   Evil spirits far off keeping.

Calmly, calmly, sweet one, rest!
   Thy young heart no sin defiling,
With thy pink hand on thy breast,
   With thy rose-cheek faintly smiling.

Brightly, brightly, I will show
   Scenes of glory to thy dreaming,
Such as man ne'er meets below,
   Paradise around thee gleaming.

Softly, softly, in heaven's bowers,
  Slumbering spirit, I will place thee;
Thou shalt pluck immortal flowers,
  And the angels shall embrace thee.

Slumber, slumber, fair-haired child,
  Type of all that's pure and holy;
God Himself on infants smiled,
  For the lofty loves the lowly.

Nearer, nearer, then I'll bend,
  As o'er streamlets hangs the willow,
And my sheltering wings extend,
  Little saint, above thy pillow.

EVENING AT HASTINGS.

Boast not of long-drawn vales and flowery plains,
  Of sounding cataracts and mountains lone;
Behold this ocean where soft beauty reigns,
  And awful grandeur to no landscape known!
The soul floats o'er yon vast expanse of sea,
And feels thy meaning, dread eternity!

The sun in fire hangs o'er the western billow,
  And every tremulous wave his mirror seems;
He rests upon a cloud, his crimson pillow,
  And there, a sleeping god, awhile he dreams;
The ships like floating gems—yon headland bold,*
Far stretching o'er the deep, a bar of gold.

And bright along the horizon's level brim,
  A rich red path is paved; the seamew's wing
Burns as it winnows ether; nought is dim,
  Save the far east where cliffs soft shadows fling,
Shadows still edged with fire; and high in air
Yon castle hangs, a ruin rent and bare.†

How silent all this mighty ocean lies !
  Hushed as an infant rocked to sleep by love,
The wavelets rosy dimples, bending skies
  A canopy; as if great Nature's dove,
Or some calm angel brooded o'er the wave,
And its own peace to Ocean's quiet gave.

There is an odour fraught with health and life,
  Wafted on shore from off the purple brine—
An odour with more living freshness rife,
  Than sweets from banks of summer eglantine;

---

* Beachy Head.   † Hastings Castle.

Drinking the spirit of the breeze-swept main,
The body and the soul new vigour gain.

Along the shingles and the yellow sand,
    Groups, idly happy, saunter, some with eyes
Cast on the deep, so lovely yet so grand,
    And others watch the west's oft-changing dyes;
And there young lovers wander, slow, apart,
That scene of beauty melting o'er each heart.

The little trim-sail'd barks are outward gliding,
    Noiseless as spirits, and the dipping oar
Breaks the tinged sapphire; anchored ships are riding
    Waves fret and die in sparkles on the shore;
At times soft singing from afar is borne,
Or floats upon the air the mellow horn.

From crowded cities and their tumult stealing,
    How soothing to the spirit wandering here !
The world another aspect is revealing,
    Earth seems transformed into a calmer sphere;
Sunset, shore, ocean, Nature's glorious whole
May well, in dreams Elysian, lap the soul.

TO-MORROW.

To-morrow—short the vista to it leading,
    And ofttimes fair;
But trust it not, the present rather heeding,
    Be that thy care.

To-morrow—stand not idly waiting, ever
    Work, work, to-day!
Improve the hour, the past returneth never;
    Madness delay.

The God-giv'n present we can boast of only,
    The morrows lie
Beyond those mountains, shadowy, dark, and lonely—
    Doubt, mystery.

R

To-morrow—some disaster may o'ertake us,
    Blighting life's flowers;
With one rude shock dear fortune may forsake us,
    Want, ruin, ours.

Kind heaven the future from man's wisdom veileth,
    Curtained each ray;
But hope's high beacon, burning, never faileth,
    Lighting our way.

To-morrow—ne'er put off thy present duty
    To that to-morrow;
Delay, a luring and Circean beauty,
    Plunging in sorrow.

Oh, the to-morrow! it may come, soft-creeping,
    With balmiest air,
Or bring the spirit tempests, whelming, sweeping,
    Wreck and despair.

Who dares exclaim, to-morrow no rich blessing
    My heart will miss?
What now I have, I still shall be possessing—
    Wealth, friends, and bliss.

Pause, mortal, though to-day the wine-cup quaffing,
    Perchance, the morrow
Will close for ever all thy feasting, laughing,
    In gloom and sorrow.

Those grasping trifles, chasing the bright present,
    With panting breath,
To-morrow, called from all things evanescent,
    May mate with death.

O guilt, repent this hour, crime's cup down-dashing;
    For thee, for thee,
To-morrow ne'er may dawn, upon thee flashing
    Eternity.

THE SOLDIER'S WIDOW AND THE PORTRAIT.

[Suggested by a painting, in which a lady, in widow's weeds, is represented gazing on the portrait of a military man.]

Reflex of one to memory dear,
    Unchanging shadow of the dead!
He looks as talking, smiling here,
    And not for ever fled:
Oh, art, kind art, to keep before us
    All that the greedy tomb would take!
And though the soul it can't restore us,
    It bids the past awake.
Portrait! those life-like features tell
    A tale of bliss no more to be;
Thou bind'st my spirit by a spell;
    I have but thee, but thee!

At first I could not lift mine eyes,
    Bowed by my new o'erwhelming grief,
But stood beneath thee, sobs and sighs
    Bringing me no relief;
But now I view that dear, calm face,
    With milder feelings, chastened woe;
I love each lineament to trace,
    And though the tear will flow,
Sweet memories pour upon my heart,
    My living love I seem to see;
With all things I would gladly part,
    Keeping but thee, but thee.

When trifling, worldly cares molest,
    And follies lure the soul and eye,
I turn to thee, and soon at rest
    Cares and temptations lie:
Not yet to crushing time I bow,
    My hair not yet is lined with gray,
But if a smile would win me now,
    Or steal my heart away,
Dear Portrait! to that nobler face,
    Reviving early faith, I flee;
All thoughts of others then I chase,
    Kept true by thee, by thee!

THE BLIND GIRL.

They tell her of an azure, arching sky,
  And a great sun that floods it all with light;
Their words are meaningless; she lifts her eye,
  But all is empty night;
And so she droops the lids with bitter sigh,
  Praying to God for sight.

They tell her of the forest-rustling hills,
  And the green vales where wander sedgy streams,
And the vast sea which man with wonder fills;
  Such pictures are but dreams:
No beauty-image her veiled spirit thrills,
  Black, black, Creation seems.

They tell her of the countless flowers that bloom,
  And preach of God, in meadow and on plain;
She feels their petals, drinks their rich perfume,
  But oh! their hues are vain!
To her the laughing garden is a tomb,
  Flower-glories yield a pain.

Dear heaven, while lifting up that brow so bright,
　How oft the fair young girl hath heaved a sigh,
That mercy one brief hour would grant her sight,
　To feast on earth and sky,
To know the meaning of that wonder—light;
　Then happy would she die.

She turned her forehead to the warming sun,
　Then to her pallid lips her flow'rets pressed;
She bent her head and sighed, like one undone,
　Hopeless, uncheered, unblest;
She bent her head and sighed, while tears begun
　To drop upon her breast.

Hark ! 'twas the blackbird's voice; his flutings came
　From the near thicket; quickly you might trace
A change in those pale features; pleasure's flame
　Broke o'er her meaning face,
And, as she blest the tuneful songster's name,
　Tears to bright smiles gave place.

Yes, Nature's simplest music breathed a spell,
　Charming, when nothing else could charm her woe;
On those sweet notes heart, fancy, seemed to dwell—
　Notes dropp'd with golden flow;
Let not e'en blindness say to joy farewell,
　While music thrills below.

THE FOUNTAIN OF THE SWEET AND BITTER.

There flows no fountain in this world of ours,
  So bright, alluring, sweet unto the lip,
Dancing in sunshine, fringed by honeyed flowers,
  Where ardent youth still deems it bliss to sip,
Gladdening earth's scenes, and mirroring scenes above,
As the smooth, lucid stream of happy love.

And yet this fountain gushes oft in gloom,
  And bears a bitterness within its tide;
For myrtle and for roses' fragrant bloom,
  Dark plants of pain o'erhang its mournful side;
Taste not, shun carefully the dangerous brink;
Yet eager votaries oft will stoop and drink.

Flow on, flow on, exhaustless fount of love!
  Without thy bitterness a precious stream;
The parent river waters plains above,
  Those crystal waves through Paradise that gleam:

Lore, science, may exalt, but, wanting thee,
How dull, how barren, all life's paths would be !

Yet love, thou art a riddle, making strong
   And all heroic, hearts most frail before ;
Now scattering resolutions, and along
   Bearing resolves—weak foam on reason's shore ;
Blinding the keen-eyed sage's boasted sight,
Casting down wisdom, and defying might.

Source of great bliss and grief—of happy smiles,
   And tears which, like slow drops that fall on stone,
Can wear the heart away ; thy sparkling wiles
   Around some spirits like a summer thrown ;
With all thy pains, thy sweets that can decoy,
We hail thee still, a blessing and a joy.

Then fountain, bright-waved fountain ! sweep and flow
   Adown the ages, gladdening human hearts !
Few weary pilgrims, finding joy or woe,
   But taste thy waters ere life's day departs ;
They ne'er will fail ; souls live though bodies die ;
Love's stream shall murmur through eternity.

THE CRY OF THE UNRESIGNED.

Come back! come back! my lost, my loved, my own!
    Too soon hath cruel death
    Stopt my young darling's breath,
Too soon her heavenly soul to heaven hath flown.
    The flowers so prized by thee,
    The softly chiming sea,
    The brook whose voice was dear,
    The birds you loved to hear,
Singing in noon's white rays, to me now black—
Join with my soul, and cry—come back! come back!

It may be impious, may be cruel too,
    But from the bowers above
    Where thou, like some white dove,
Dost sit in purity amidst the blue,
    To earth I'd bring thee down,
    Nor heed thy amaranth crown;
    Any thing in my madness,
    Any thing in my sadness,

So I could have thee near,
Fold thee, and kiss thee, dear:
O angels, hear me! bear her down yon track
Of luminous stars—lost child! come back! come back

Whether I sit alone at morn or night,
Praying to be resigned,
Strengthening with hope my mind,
Striving to chase thee from my inner sight;
In vain; still thought will fly
To blissful days gone by;
Anguish doth tear my soul,
The tempest mocks control;
I rail at fate, my spirit on a rack,
And still I cry—sweet saint! come back! come back!

To my fond soul thou wert a vernal sun;
I warmed in thee, loved child,
Thy beams so softly mild;
My thoughts from thee, poor flowers, their fragrance won;
Now all is night, blind night,
Set my dear orb of light;
Friends strive in vain to cheer me,
Thou, thou no longer near me;
In darkness thick I grope,
Without my sun, my hope,

Still calling on thee, though in joy—and black
This lower world to thine—come back! come back!

I loved thee stronger as time winged his flight,
      Engrossingly and madly;
      All virtues seemed to clad thee;
Thy mother's voice, her eyes of sunniest light:
      And thou didst also love me,
      Though beautiful, above me,
      As rainbow o'er a hill;
      Thy soul I worship still,
      But oh, I crave more, more—
      To have thee on life's shore,
To hear thee, fold thee, kiss thee—down the track
Of yonder blue, descend! come back! come back!

THE LOVED AND LOST.

Where are they now, the loved but long departed,
    The gentle, true, and kind,
Who left us on life's road, foot-worn, sad-hearted,
    With wounds time scarce may bind?

Where are they now? abroad when we may wander,
    Do they beside us move,
Mourn when we mourn, reflect, too, when we ponder,
    Answering, unmarked, our love?

Or when within our silent chamber seated,
    We think of days long o'er,
Come they unseen, unheard, and are we greeted
    By their dear lips once more?

Haunt they the valley once so loved, adoring
    God in the beauteous flowers,
Listening to rills, and birds joy-anthems pouring,
    Charmed as in mortal hours?

Wander their spirits by the sounding ocean,
    Reading in storms heaven's might,
Feeling 'mid glorious scenes sublime devotion,
    Raised to thought's loftiest height?

Or on the clouds of splendour are they floating,
    When sunset fires the skies,
The opal gates, and golden paths, denoting
    The way to paradise?

Or have they ris'n to yonder star, whose whiteness
    Of purity doth tell,
Walking in loveliness the hills of brightness—
    Land where no sorrows dwell?

Where are they now? oh, where? the lost, the vanished,
    Love's cords of silver riven;
Near or afar, on earth or ever banished,
    Enough! they are in heaven.

And where that heaven? if in the blue above us,
    Depths of eternal rest,
Or in some orb which, shining, seems to love us;
    Enough that they are blest.

MYLOR CHURCH AND FALMOUTH HARBOUR,

CORNWALL.

'Tis not when jocund morning walks the hills,
   Scattering dew-pearls, and laughing o'er the sea;
Or when bright noon the glen with sunshine fills,
   And birds pipe jubilee,
That thou shouldst visit Mylor's pensive shades,
View creek and shore, and tread its leafy glades.

But when eve, Nature's artist, paints the west,
   With many a ruby line and orange ray,
Striving to make a gorgeous couch of rest
   For sleepy, weary day;
And quiet lulls the hills and woods of green;
Then feels the heart the magic of the scene.

'Tis now that hour; I gaze across the wave,
    Burnished and glossy in the crimson light;
The pebbly beach the little billows lave,
    In thin-drawn lines of white,
Pulsing with sounds most faint the evening air,
As if from ocean's heart there breathed a prayer.

Oh, beautiful the circling hills that gird
    Fal's sheltering harbour! 'mid wild storms of fear,
Safe in her nest as sits the brooding bird,
    The great ship rideth here:
Fair-walled Trelissick decks the green hill's side,
And down each bank woods sloping kiss the tide.

The castles* guard the waters far away,
    But oft their stirring thunders swell the breeze;
St. Just's smooth uplands catch the dying ray,
    While gold bathes all the trees:
White cottages are sprinkled o'er each steep,
Like drifts of snow, the flocks of nibbling sheep.

---

* Pendennis and St. Mawes Castles, built in the reign of
Henry VIII. The former stands on an elevation upwards of
300 feet above the sea, and commands a prospect as extensive
and beautiful as any to be seen on the Cornish coasts.

But Mylor's old grey church and rugged tower,
  Unchanged amid a thousand changeful years,
Attract my steps; how solemn, this calm hour,
  The ancient pile appears !
Link between us and darkling ages fled,
A something holy watching o'er the dead.

The tottering belfry thickest ivies hide,
  A pall hung o'er it by funereal time;
How often up the glens, across the tide,
  Hath swung that bell's soft chime !
Yes, it hath tolled through ages; now you hear
A small sweet trill; the redbreast carols near.

Mylor, beneath thy famed and mighty yew,
  That gives death's dwellings beauty, let me stand ;
The solemn and the lovely meet my view,
  A charm on sea and land:
O Nature ! thy sweet aspects soften gloom,
And kindly chase the terror of the tomb.

Here generations have renounced the dreams
  That filled each busy brain in long-past day;
Here grief forgets its tears, and craft its schemes,
  The gleesome child its play,

The village maid her conquests, here to close
Her sprightly laughing eyes in calm repose.

By yon rude stone where lengthening shadows fall,
  The honest peasant rests to plough no more;
In that white tomb, once courted, loved by all,
  The squire's career is o'er;
Beneath where leaves low whisper like a brook,
The priest for ever now hath closed his book.

Yew, venerable, sombre, stately tree!
  Sure thou dost droop in grief, and vigil keep
Beside the mound where, victims of the sea,
  A hundred warriors sleep:
For fields of blood, for cannon's thunder-boom,
Above their heads now white-ruffed daisies bloom.*

Sweet resting-place, past mortal hopes and fears,
  Old church that sanctifies and guards the graves,
Yew, braving tempests through a thousand years,
  Wide, music-breathing waves!

---

* In one grave near the great yew-tree, lie interred more than
a hundred soldiers, who, returning from Spain in the "Queen"
transport-ship, at the close of the Peninsular war, were most
lamentably wrecked during a strong gale from the south, on
Trefusis Point. The harbour then had no breakwater.

Green-hanging wood, brown glen, and sloping hill—
Peace on them rest, and beauty haunt them still !

Peace too with him, whose voice so oft is hèard
  In yon gray pile, whose counsels point to heaven !
Who cheers grief, age, with many a kindly word,
  Whose alms to want are given;
Well may these lovely scenes calm bliss impart,
And nearer to his Maker draw his heart.

THE WAKING INFANT.

I GAZED upon its laughing eyes,
  That mocked the sapphire's blue,
Its cheek rich-red as ruby-dyes,
  Its lips of coral hue,
And saw its brow more fair than snow,
Ere it hath caught a taint below.

I viewed it on the couch of rest,
  With locks of curly grace;
Heaved soft as fountain-wave its breast,
  And from its seraph face

Glanced the sweet brightness of a dream,
Like sunshine from a summer stream.

It woke, and stretched its rosy arms,
    As asking a caress
From her who watched its slumbering charms—
    Oh, task of blessedness!
E'en like an angel or a dove,
To bend o'er all we prize and love.

The mother raised it on her knee,
    And danced her cherub boy;
How then burst forth its artless glee,
    All trembling as with joy,
Lips open, dimples on each cheek,
And eyes that, sparkling, seemed to speak.

Sweet thing of innocence! I sighed,
    How lovely now art thou!
Pure as a pearl in ocean's tide,
    Or dew on morning's brow:
O happy age! O golden prime!
Unfelt a care, unknown a crime.

SPARE HER, DEATH.

By her youth's unfolding spring,
When hope's flowers are blossoming;
By her beauty's sunny light,
Not yet ready for the night;
By her eye's pure liquid ray,
Not yet meant to fade away;
   Spare her, Death !

By her love for Nature's face—
Glory she delights to trace;
By her love of flowers, whose bloom
Cannot smile within the tomb;
By her joy in music's spell
Ne'er in silent vaults to swell;
   Spare her, Death !

By her tender, yearning heart,
Grieving with each friend to part;
Wishing still to pass life's hours
In a world so fair as ours;
By her shrinking from the cold,
And the dark beneath the mould;
   Spare her, Death !

By her mother's piteous weeping,
In her own her thin hand keeping,
Looking in her face so white,
And her eyes so strangely bright;
By her father's anxious fears,
By her loving sister's tears;
      Spare her, Death!

Go, and hurl thy poisoned dart
At bowed sorrow's hopeless heart!
Strike at those who long for rest
On the bed of earth's calm breast,
Aged, fading from the scene;
Here the plant is fresh and green;
      Spare her, Death!

Spare her, in her beauty, spare her!
From the warm world do not tear her;
Pity her, if thy hard heart
Ever felt keen pity's smart;
Turn thy cruel shaft away
From the lovely, youthful prey;
      Spare her, Death!

THE MAID OF THE ISLES.

THE Scilly Isles were faintly burning,
  As day's red chariot westward rolled;
The wave its dashing spray was turning
  To powdered rubies, dust of gold.

Beauty upon those rocks was beaming,
  Beauty more bright than lustrous eve;
Such vision fancy, sweetly dreaming,
  In fairyland will sometimes weave.

Slender and lithe as Spring's young willow,
  She stooped to gather samphire there;
The sun, half sleeping on his pillow,
  Woke up to view a form so fair;

And lingered, smiling warmly, brightly,
  On peach-soft cheek and rounded arms;
And as she tripp'd o'er rocks so lightly,
  He bathed in richest beams her charms.

Back from her brow dishevell'd, glowing,
  In long brown masses streamed her hair;
The breeze aside her mantle blowing,
  Her tiny feet glanced white and bare.

Her eyes now rested on the ocean—
  Great eyes that let out all the soul;
Her breast was like the wave in motion,
  As sweetest thoughts upon her stole.

Here life's young morning passed; the glory
  Of English cities—palace, tower,
To her a vague and dreamy story,
  Nought to her heart birth, pride, or power.

The vales that boasted scanty tillage,
  The venturous fisher's sail unfurled,
The wandering goats, the humble village,
  Seemed to her untaught soul—the world.

Thus grew she, nurtured 'mid the roaring
  Of that great ocean, never still,
Free as the eagle sunward soaring,
  Wild as the wild-flower on the hill.

Now see her nimbly, goat-like springing,
  As lingering day's rich smiles depart;
Now hear her like a joy-bird singing,
  In the warm summer of her heart.

O Island Beauty! would the splendour,
  Wealth, pomp, by distant lands possessed,
Thy simple life more lovely render,
  Or make thy gentle heart more blest?

THE YOUNG OPERA-DANCER.

Brightly are the stage-lights shining,
  Gay and gorgeous is the scene,
Groups of nymphs their arms are twining,
  Dancing on a festive green:

Spectacle, each sense entrancing!
　　Music making bosoms swell—
Oh, the magic of that dancing!
　　Charming with a wondrous spell.

See, beneath an arch of roses,
　　One fair maid glides forward now;
'Tis the bride—by those white posies,
　　By the pearls that crown her brow.
All fall back as she advances,
　　Bounding, graceful as the roe,
And her foot, like meteor, glances,
　　To and fro—and to and fro.

Matchless dancing—sure a fairy
　　Hath just left Titania's halls;
'Tis so joyous, sprightly, airy,
　　Snow less light than those foot-falls:
Ay, a spirit seems as burning
　　In that tiny foot, now slow,
Now, like lightning, crossing, turning,
　　To and fro—and to and fro.

Oh, the young girl's graceful springing,
　　Steps by last steps still surpassed!
Now applause is wildly ringing,
　　Bouquets round her thickly cast.

Pleased she looks, joy undissembling,
  And bright smiles her thanks express—
Yes, for very joy she's trembling;
  Sweet are plaudits, sweet success!

Wearied, listless, leans the dancer,
  After midnight in her room;
Eyes to pleasure flash no answer,
  Cheeks have lost their painted bloom:
Flowers upon the floor are lying,
  Pale, thin fingers beat her brow,
And her vacant breast is sighing,
  No glad nymph, no fairy now!

What avail applauses, only
  Given to grace, to nimble feet?
Her young heart is cold and lonely,
  No kind heart to love or greet.
Hers but toil for others' pleasure,
  Now, the poor excitement o'er,
How she loathes the gold-paid measure,
  Source of pride and bliss before!

Leaning on her hand, she's thinking
  Of her home by Como's tide,
And she views the calm sun sinking,
  And the Alps in glory dyed.

She doth feel more joy is dwelling
  In that home fond memory keeps,
Than in plaudits loudly swelling,
  And the world-praised dancer weeps.

THE MILITARY HERO.

O War ! what is it that invests thy brow
  With captivating glory ?   Through all years
Why has youth panted at thy feet to bow,
  And felt a joy in danger, mocking fears ?
Loud swell thy stirring trumpet-notes ; his eye
Burns with new flame to see thy banner fly ;
And to be called a hero, he will brave
The chance of suffering, peril, and the grave.

Say, what are laurels ? sighed-for, dazzling prize,
  Worthless, yet precious ; man would fain appear
Daring and valiant in his fellows' eyes,
  Laurels to base, as noble, spirits, dear :
They crowned Miltiades with solemn glory,
They sat on Timur's brow all dark and gory,
They wove for Cæsar everlasting fame,
But many a forehead since have seared with flame.

What now remains of ancient fields of strife,
 Great, famous in their day, where heroes fought,
And man won honour as he took man's life ?
 Ask the weird, passing winds—they answer nought;
Ask the wild flowers that deck the shrunken graves,
Ask Cannæ's plain and Granicus' red waves;
Nature forgets them, fear hath ceased to bow,—
Their agony and glory nothing now.

Thou mighty shaker of the moral world,
 And changer of the destinies of man !
Let thy proud standard joyous be unfurled,
 Let crimson-handed slaughter lead the van;
Burn and destroy ! rise, plume-crowned terror ! rise !
Alluring honour flashing in thine eyes;
Thou eldest born of passion ! mount thy car
By furies drawn, O hydra-headed War !

Ambition still will follow thee, and pride
 Behold but glory in thy ghastly mien;
Pomp and excitement still thy horrors hide,
 And throw a magic o'er each bloody scene :
What are bereavements, widows', orphans' sighs ?
For victory won, men's thanks to heaven arise;
To heal a feud, when words might healers be,
The sword sweeps thousands to eternity.

———————

NIGHT BY THE CORNISH COAST.

ANGEL of light! cast down thy flaming torch,
And quench it in yon ocean, cold and deep!
Come forth, star-vestals! who all day have prayed,
Hidden within your cloister-cells of heaven;
Unveil your pearly brows, unclose your eyes,
And unabashed look down, that earth may drink
Your pure celestial beauty: abbess moon!
Sit 'mid your docile nuns, nor with cold gaze
Check their coy twinkling smiles, so sweet to-night.
Thou sleepy sea! smooth out each curling wave,
Burnish its face, and edge it with soft silver,
To make a glass, that ocean's wandering nymphs
May see their faces, and braid up their hair.—
Rest in your cradle-caves, ye infant winds,
That else might grow to storms!—Steal, silence! forth
From night's blue chamber, and with finger laid
On Nature's lip, walk soft the water-world;

And beauty! with bare arms and ivory brow,
Glide on the beam from heaven's starr'd paradise,
And breathe on shore, and deep, and pine-topp'd hill,
Your spell of grace and glory.—Night! O night!
The calmer and exalter! earth and man,
And all that's lovely, owe a debt to thee.
The conscious ocean from its stilled deep breast,
Through its fresh lips—the murmuring shelly shore—
Cries out—I love thee, night!—The mountain-tops,
Shimmering and smiling 'neath heaven's lamp-like stars,
Exclaim—I love thee, night!—The haunted vale,
Half-sleeping, half-awake—delicious trance—
With all its freshened woods, and dew-hung flowers,
And silvery rills, whispers—I love thee, night!
Let, too, the soul of man that would in peace
Muse or aspire, and sweet communion hold
With God and Nature, cry—I love thee, night!

EARLY MORNING IN REGENT'S PARK.

The mighty city still is in repose,
Sleep laps its feverish joys, its anxious woes,
Labour's great hammer strikes not yet its blows.

The myriad chimneys have not yet begun
Sending up household smoke to veil the sun,
And skies are blue where all will soon be dun.

Though near the vast metropolis, I seem
In some still country place, and cannot dream,
That yonder spreads life's turbid, troubled stream.

Autumn's broad sun shines golden o'er the trees,
The yellowing leaves hang crisply in the breeze,
And o'er the grass low hum the tawny bees.

Warmth to the flowret's cheek the beams are bringing,
The last few butterflies abroad are winging,
Earlier than man awake, the lark is singing.

With paddling feet, and arching neck of snow,
The swan her sail commences, graceful, slow,
The water with her beauty all a-glow.

And little fish are darting, sporting there,
Woo'd upwards by the sun and freshening air,
Life unto them one morn, without a care.

I scent from yon enclosure* rich perfume,
Where foreign flowers of every hue and bloom
Weave robes for peris in bright Nature's loom.

There palms lift high their heads to catch the beam,
And oranges on trees, red blushes, gleam,
Till they who gaze, in Orient countries seem.

Hark! wakened by the early cheerful ray,
Barr'd in their countless cages far away,†
I hear strange birds—the scream and softened lay.

I hear the eagle's cry, again to soar
To you bright sun, though doomed to mount no more;
The wolf's low howl—the restless tiger's roar.

---

* The Botanical Gardens.　　† The Zoological Gardens.

Thus drinking morning's breath, and looking through
The quivering boughs on heaven's pure crystal blue,
Gladness and health where'er I turn my view;

I will not think that scarce a mile away
A populous city lies, which soon will sway
With wildering tumult, ushering in the day.

That soon thro' long, long streets will press the throng,
The wagon creak, the horseman dash along,
And lusty life sing loud its deafening song.

I seem as much alone on this green sod,
With Nature's soothing spirit and her God,
As if some desert isle, or waste I trod.

Heaven speaks in gentlest whispers from on high,
I view dew-beaded grass, the trees, the sky,
And from deep Nature's heart there breathes one sigh;

The sigh of half-suppressed, half-gushing bliss,
That she is free the varied earth to kiss,
Blooming near dust-dark cities fair as this.

THE TOWER OF LONDON.

Fort, prison, palace! 'mid thy towers we wander,
  Where strength, like Samson, mourns its glory fled;
O what a crowd of memories, while we ponder,
  Bursts, ghost-like, from the graves of ages dead!

Since the proud Conqueror laid these strong foundations,
  What blood has here been spilt! what bitter showers
Of tears poor eyes have rain'ed! what sad creations
  Fancy has bodied in yon prison-towers!

The Traitor's Gate—through these now silent portals,
  How many victims, pale and shivering, passed!
Guilty and innocent—worst, best of mortals,
  Here on the outer world have looked their last.

Now warders, up and down, are calmly walking,
　Scenting the ancient stones, sweet wall-flowers
　　blow :
Cannons are rusting, men are idly talking,
　Nor care for anguish felt long years ago.

But had yon Beauchamp Tower the gift of speaking,*
　Each room, each stone, a tale of grief would tell,
Of hopes for ever blasted, fond hearts breaking;
　Oh, man oft makes for man an earthly hell !

Still on the darkened walls we read inscriptions,
　Traced by the agonised in hopeless hours—
Love—prayers for strength—but nowhere maledictions;
　Brave men, fair women—long, long faded flowers !

---

* Sir Walter Raleigh was confined in the White Tower, but the greatest number of illustrious victims were imprisoned in the Beauchamp Tower, some of the walls of which are covered with inscriptions. From this tower many famous men and women were taken to execution, some being beheaded in front of St. Peter's Chapel, and others on Tower Hill. For a graphic account of one of the most interesting periods of the history of the Tower, see Mr. Hepworth Dixon's work, "*Her Majesty's Tower*," and Mr. Ainsworth's romance.

I stand before the Chapel; let me travel
　　Back through the ages—what a scene is there!
The young, the beautiful *—those curls unravel;
　　Pause, headsman, while they shear her golden
　　　　hair!

Around her eyes the bandage she is tying,
　　Her last warm prayer, forgiveness for her foes;
Now on the block her beauteous head is lying—
　　A flashing stroke ends all her pangs and woes!

To heaven's bright gate I see her soul ascending,
　　For mortal crowns a brighter crown above,
And seraphs from the clouds are smiling, bending,
　　Whispering sweet peace and everlasting love.

But other spirits, sufferers famed and glorious,
　　Have here sprung upwards from their blood-stained
　　　　biers,
And, great as warriors falling when victorious,
　　They claim our reverence, while they ask our tears.

---

* Lady Jane Grey.

All, all is quiet now; the past's deep ocean
   Rolls o'er those buried days; the wind's faint
    breath
Whispers to yonder flag in tremulous motion—
   No cruel law gives now the just to death.

The sun, while dying west, is calmly throwing
   O'er all the fortress, crimson, slanting beams,
And in the light each rugged tower is glowing,
   Like age which smiles when sleep brings youthful
    dreams.

An ancient clock the fleeting hour is telling,
   The sentinel is pacing idly-slow;
The hum of London drowsily is swelling;
   The spot is peace—no more a scene of woe.

THE MYSTERY OF MUSIC.

Call not music mere vibrations,
　　Pulsing, trembling, floating by,
Just to raise pleased, brief sensations,
　　Fruitless sounds but born to die.

No, it is a spirit burning,
　　Subtile, lightning-like, in air;
Dormant it may lie, till turning
　　A true, living spirit there:

Wakened by the throat's fine quiver,
　　By the harp, or horn, or lyre:
God to charm us was the giver
　　Of this air-born thing of fire.

O the power of warblings golden,
　　Of a soft or mighty tone !
Men bowed down in ages olden,
　　And still bend at music's throne.

Earth contains no savage nation,
　　Where sweet sounds touch not the soul;
E'en the unreasoning, brute creation
　　Owns their strong and strange control.

Serpents, drawn by music, listen,
　　Birds glad warble unto birds,
And their quick eyes brightly glisten,
　　Songs their rich melodious words.

What doth cheer us when we languish,
　　Like the gush of simple lays ?
What doth soothe us when in anguish,
　　Like the songs of happier days ?

Think not music swelling, pealing,
　　Or soft breathing dulcet sighs,
Making molten hardest feeling,
　　Lifting earth-thoughts to the skies,

Perishes when past—Oh, never !
  Science tells us each sweet tone
Must swell on, sweep on for ever,
  E'en to God's high, distant throne.

SUMMER IS COME.

Summer is come; her eye is glowing
  From out heaven's depths of cloudless blue,
In music sun-kissed streams are flowing,
  And winds are warm, but fragrant too.
Loud pipes the thrush, a rapture feeling
  In Nature's joy; upsprings more high
The russet lark, in circles wheeling,
  To cool his pinions in the sky.

Summer is come; on plain and mountain,
  I see her walk with rosy feet;
She sleeks her bright locks in the fountain,
  Her purple zone unbound for heat;

Beneath her soft step flowers are springing,
   Of richest breath, and loveliest dyes,
Delighted bees around them winging,
   While fairies drink their odorous sighs.

Summer is come; I see her flushing
   On garden wall, in poppied dale;
The cherry 'neath green leaves is blushing,
   Like some coy maid behind her veil.
Down in the dell where brooks are brawling,
   To lave their hoofs the cattle stray;
The cuckoo from the wood is calling,
   And merrily maidens toss the hay.

Summer is come; the heart rejoices,
   With livelier bound the pulses beat;
From Nature's haunts a thousand voices
   The flower-crowned, laughing goddess greet:
Oh, say not earth, grown dark and hoary,
   No trace of Paradise retains;
She mirrors back lost Eden's glory,
   To bless our souls, while Summer reigns.

THE SPIRIT OF RUIN.

WHEN man was banished Eden's bowers,
  I sprang to dark and dreaded birth;
The sparkling springs, the new-born flowers,
  I dimmed, I crushed in mocking mirth:
I shook the glittering crystal walls,
  And where bright birds, with starry wings,
Sang to the diamond waterfalls,
  And wandered gentlest, loveliest things,
I brought the vulture, tiger, snake,
  To prey and rend, to howl and hiss;
Poisons I planted in each brake—
  Sweet to mine eyes a scene like this.
Ay, revel on, and proudly shine,
Exulting earth! thou'rt mine, thou'rt mine!

O'er Babylon I spread my plume;
  Her brazen gates, her gardens fair,
Her sceptred kings, received their doom—
  A voiceless waste now darkens there.

I sped to Salem's sacred tower,
    Smiled on the smiling, haughty Jew;
Her blazing Temple owned my power,
    My trumpet on her walls I blew.
Memphis that shone by Nile's broad wave,
    And Tadmor making deserts gay,
Carthage that laws to nations gave—
    I stretched my wand, and where were they?
Yes, revel on, and proudly shine,
Cities of earth! you're mine, you're mine!

To Europe next I wing'd my flight;
    On Græcia's shore, 'neath sunny skies,
I saw, in marble beauty bright,
    The statue smile, the pillar rise:
By Pallas' shrine I took my stand,
    And viewed the column'd plain below;
Ne'er was a scene more proud and grand,
    Ne'er did more beauty burn and glow.
I raised my phial, slowly poured
    Its poison-drops on Athens' head;
Those drops were ages, flood, and sword—
    Her temples sank, her glory fled;
All, all, except her poet's line,
Yielded to time's dark spell, and mine!

My home is now by Tiber's tide;
  I watch the seven-hilled city fall;
Daily I crush some arch of pride,
  And chant my song in Cæsar's hall.
And from that site of fallen power,
  Northward at times I speed my way,
To robe with moss some feudal tower,
  And in young cities plant decay.
And when wars fail, with ages slow,
  To bow their pride, I waste with fire;
I laugh 'mid shrieks of human woe,
  And clap my hands o'er each red pyre;
My joy, my strength, shall ne'er decline,
All, save man's soul, is mine, is mine!

A REVERIE AMONG THE ALPS.

I GAZE upon those masses, lifting high
   Their brows like an eternity in stone,
To hold communion with the bending sky—
   Those speakers in the infinite alone,
Whose words are tempests, and whose glances fire,
Darting from clouds electric round each spire.
Sure mountains breathe, like ocean's solemn roll,
Nature's sublime religion o'er the soul.

Lo! Rosa standeth with his shield of snow,
   His giant breast all mailed with iron frost;
Tempests may rave, and lightnings flash below,
   Defying all, his spear on high is tost;
He shouts to Cenis, whose cloud-flag unfurls,
And wrathful Viso, who his av'lanche hurls,
While Jungfrau, battling in his icy car,
His cannon-voice of thunder sounds afar.

The king above his subjects calmly sits,
  Majestic as stupendous and alone;
The wandering cloud, like some small insect, flits
  Around the pillars of his steadfast throne:
Mont Blanc looks forth in mightiness, his eye
Claims nothing worthy of him save the sky,
Owns, raised like an archangel o'er the sod,
Only one higher, Him who made him—God.

Have mountains language?   Yes, they speak to man
  With tongues ne'er mute through long-revolving
    time—
Grand poems writ, when Nature's youth began,
  By God's own finger, glorious and sublime.
Mountains to teach humility were given,
Mountains are spirits' stepping-stones to heaven;
They rose 'mid dread convulsions, storms, and thunder,
A pride, a fear, a beauty, and a wonder.

NATURE'S MORNING HYMN OF PRAISE.

Thou sun, upspringing in thy car of light,
   Whose wheels are opal rays,
Chasing the demon-shadows of the night,
   Life in thy burning gaze!
For strength renewed, shout on the flaming height,
   Thy glorious Maker's praise!

Ye rivers in the beam that flash and bound!
   Rills, harp-like tinklings given!
Great sea, that roll'st the mighty world around,
   Your waves by tempests driven,
Pealing your organ with exalting sound—
   Each raise a song to heaven!

Ye flowers that open dewy, joyous eyes,
  Past the deep sleep of night!
For richer sweets, for fresher, lovelier dyes,
  Tints, Nature's blushes bright,
Breathe forth your thanks in odours to the skies,
  Sing praise with lips of light!

Thou lark, spire upwards from thy heathy bed,
  Shaking thy wings of brown!
For beauty on the earth, and light o'erhead,
  Pour thy glad song-shower down;
Trill thanks to Him who glory's feast has spread,
  Smiling off Nature's frown.

Ye winds that fan green plains, and drink perfume,
  From every wilding flower,
That pierce the rustling forest's solemn gloom,
  Or sigh 'round beauty's bower,
Murmur soft anthems down the vales of bloom,
  Praise God for this sweet hour!

Mountains, and streams, and dells, and ocean hoar!
  All Nature peans raise,
To Him whose bounty blesses earth once more!
  All sounds be turned to lays!
Man, man, take up the strain! your God adore,
  And grateful chant His praise.

KATHERINE SOUTHEY.

IN MEMORIAM.

Miss Katherine Southey died at Laithwaite Cottage, near Keswick, on the 8th August, 1864, and was buried under the shadows of Mount Skiddaw. She was the third daughter of the late Robert Southey, and the last surviving member of his family.

LAST daughter of the bard—
Of him, the sage and good, whose honoured name
Doth shine serenely in the sky of fame;
A bard that in his wreath twined virtue's flower,
　　Which sweetly breathes a living fragrance still;
Whose mem'ry, like a grey and ivied tower,
　　The years make strong, adorns Time's misty hill.

Last child of Southey's love;
Who, when an infant, prattled in his ear,
The youngest still to parent's heart most dear;

She watched his progress, and, in life's decay,
  Smoothed his white hair, and checked the weary sigh,.
And with another,* death has snatched away,
  Tended his wants, and closed his dying eye.

Last scion of the bard;
She sleeps where Nature weaves her loveliest spells,
Romance sits queen, and calm-eyed beauty dwells;
Where Greta murmurs her weird evening song,
  And Derwentwater spreads, another sky,
And Skiddaw's mighty shadow falls along
  The grassy mound where low her relics lie.

Southey's last lingering flower;
Day slowly fadeth in the yellow west,
And on her grave the warming sunbeams rest;
The speedwell turns to court the sinking ray,
  The bee goes home, the bat is whirring near,
The plaintive redbreast pipes a farewell lay;
  Nature doth know no death, still lovely here.

Last daughter of the bard;
He loved e'en with a passion this sweet scene,
Hoar rock, the mountain side, the meadow green;

---

* Southey's second wife, Miss Bowles, the authoress.

His music song of birds and splash of rills,
　His heart, attuned by God, to rapture given;
Say, doth his shade still roam these dear-loved hills?
　Oh, no; beyond the stars, he rests in heaven.

Last child of Southey's love;
Her spirit to that heaven and him has fled,
Yet on her grave shall memory's tear be shed;
Long shall this scene recall her father's name—
　Scene sweetly peaceful, beautifully wild,
Lake, glen, and mountain, linked with Southey's fame,
　Whose light, a halo, rests upon the child.

MOURN NOT.

Mourn not—through Nature's wide domain,
　Nought droops in hopeless woe;
The flowers in gladness prank the plain,
　The streamlets dancing flow;
The sun wheels up, and laughs away
　Night's frown from off the world;
Birds blithely hymn their heaven-taught lay;
　Then grief's black flag be furled!

While Nature's throbbing heart is glad,
Shall godlike man alone be sad?

Mourn not when first the infant's eyes
   On earth's dark scenes unclose;
A stranger come to breathe life's sighs,
   And wrestle with its woes;
But deem a wondrous thing has birth,
   One more high race begun;
Mind, heaven-aspiring mind, has worth,
   Surpassing star or sun;
A world may end by God's decree,
But soul shall never cease to be.

Mourn not for manhood doomed to spend
   Hard years in toil and strife,
That nightshade with hope's flowers must blend—
   Rough, rough the road of life:
Trials but make more pure the heart,
   By woe are lessons taught;
Up! what were valour's boasted part,
   No battle to be fought?
Did lightnings flash not, storms ne'er rave,
Disease would brood on land and wave.

Mourn not that time will take no rest,
With feathered feet onsweeping,
That life's sun seeks so soon the west,
Dim twilight round us creeping ;
Honour shall crown the head of snow,
Old age still rev'rence claim ;
The soul more strong, more wise shall grow,
As feebler bends the frame,
And brighten in that lustre cast
From skies it hopes to reach at last.

SHORT POEMS.

DESIGNED FOR MUSIC.

DOES LOVE DWELL IN YONDER STAR?

DOES love dwell in yonder star,
   Beaming with so soft a ray,
Angels watching it afar,
   Singing on its radiant way?
Does the heart love's transports know,
   Anxious hopes, in that sweet sphere,
All its joy, and all its woe,
   Such as swell the bosom here?

In yon planet bright and fair,
   Are there balmy evening hours?
Has heaven made for lovers there
   Whispering brooks, and blooming flowers?
Do they roam, in fragrant Spring,
   Through green vales 'neath rustling trees?
Do glad birds to charm them sing?
   Do bells murmur on the breeze?

Yes, sweet Nature smiles and glows,
　　All her beauties bless that sphere,
All we know that planet knows,
　　Save pain's sigh and sorrow's tear :
Yes, love dwells in yonder star,
　　Beaming with so soft a ray,
Angels watching it afar,
　　Singing on its radiant way.

THE WORLD OF FLOWERS.

Flowers are the jewels given to gleam
　　On Nature's flowing, gorgeous dress;
Flowers are the artists of the beam,
　　Painting our world with loveliness;
Flowers, bright-eyed flowers! their breath divine
　　To sorrow's heart will yield a bliss;
Whate'er in loftier worlds may shine,
　　O give me flowers, sweet flowers in this!

Flowers are the censers breathing sweets
　　Back to the sun for warmth and light;
Flowers are the maidens whom he greets,
　　Making them blush in coy delight:

What were the earth without bright flowers,
    Those gems dropt sparkling from above?
Dull as a heart in human bowers,
    Deprived of friendship and of love.

Flowers ever chase our thoughts of gloom,
    And oh, they shine so pure, so fair,
On heaven's own plains they sure might bloom,
    Or deck an angel's golden hair.
Flowers, bright-eyed flowers! their breath divine
    To sorrow's heart will yield a bliss;
Whate'er in loftier worlds may shine,
    O give me flowers, sweet flowers in this!

SOMETHING WE MUST LOVE.

Something, something, we must love;
    Though the heart would fling
Soft affection to the winds,
    Grown an icy thing;
Yet beneath the bosom's frost,
    Feeling's snow-drops spring.

Something, something, we must love;
   Friend may turn to foe,
We may spurn at proffer'd joy,
   Bitter made by woe;
Yet on something—bird or flower,
   Love we must bestow.

Something, something, we must love;
   So the man of pride,
Crime-stain'd, prison'd weary years,
   Nought to love beside,
Loved the spider in his cell,
   Weeping when it died.

Something, something, we must love;
   Who can chain free will?
Quench affection? roses crush,
   Sweets they yet distil;
Lone, forsaken, some poor thing
   We must cling to still.

OUR BEAUTIFUL WORLD.

Our beautiful world!   Oh, wrong
  To paint it in darkness and age!
Nature carols a joyous song,
  And laughs at the sad-hearted sage:
The sun beams as brightly on high,
  And flowers smile as sweetly around,
As when he first blazed in the sky,
  As when they first scented the ground.

Our beautiful world!   Still the Spring
  Comes tripping in freshness and mirth;
Warm Summer shakes joy from her wing,
  Rich Autumn makes golden the earth:
Nurse Winter a cradle bends o'er,
  Rocking Nature to sleep for awhile,
That man may enjoy her the more,
  When she wakes with a bright, happy smile.

Our beautiful world!   God's power
  Preserves what He loveth so dear;
Had man such perfection this hour,
  We should walk a Paradise here.

Our beautiful world !   Oh, wrong
    To paint it in darkness and age !
Nature carols a joyous song,
    And laughs at the sad-hearted sage.

THE LANGUAGE OF THE BELLS.

BELLS ! with your loud defiant notes,
    Of victory proudly telling,
A spirit in your music floats,
    Exultant, booming, swelling :
Bells ! when the new year springs to birth,
    Out from the steeple ringing,
Ye sound like hope's sweet voice to earth,
    A happier era bringing.

Bells ! through the fragrant morning air,
    Sending your merry voices,
Ye murmur of a wedded pair,
    While every heart rejoices :
Ye speak of bosoms bounding light,
    Thus swelling, rising, pealing,
Of a long future blest and bright,
    Love's vows with music sealing.

Bells ! from the tower so old and gray,
   At evening softly swinging,
Bidding adieu to dying day,
   The thrush in concert singing;
Ye summon from the tombs of years
   Memories long darkly lying,
Until our eyes o'erflow with tears,
   Our words are lost in sighing.

THE STAR-WORSHIPPER.

Hail ! lamp of beauty burning
   O'er perished daylight's bier !
To thee love's brow is turning,
   The light he deems most dear :
Sparkle, thou gem, the rarest
   Hewn from the mines of space !
Of all the diamonds fairest,
   Night's coronet that grace.

Unclose, thou eye of brightness !
   Whose lids have shut all day;
Smile through those locks of lightness,
   The clouds that 'round thee stray.

How sweet to watch thee beaming,
  Fair star, in yon abyss!
Thou seem'st, to fancy's dreaming,
  A lovelier world than this.

Then smile, thou orb of glory!
  And charm our vision here;
Sleeping on mountains hoary,
  Gilding the night-flower's tear.
Sparkle, thou gem, the rarest
  Hewn from the mines of space!
Of all the diamonds fairest,
  Night's coronet that grace.

WHEN MOST DO I THINK OF THEE?

WHEN most do I think of thee,
  My brave one in distant land?
Not when sunshine is smiling on me,
  And friends around me stand:
Not in wildering, noisy streets,
  Nor in crowds where laughter is heard,
Where the heart no true heart meets,
  And no tender emotion is stirred.

When most do I think of thee?
'Tis at evening's silent hour,
When memory's angel with me
Sits awake in her starry bower;
When she paints past blissful days,
Then I feel thee wanting, love;
O'er the wide, wide sea I gaze,
Then I weep thy absence, love.

When most do I think of thee?
'Tis when cares overcast life's skies,
And none can my comforters be,
And the heart in its bitterness sighs:
Like some bird that pines for its nest,
To thy bosom I then would flee;
There only the wife can rest;
Yes, in grief I think chiefly of thee.

THE VALLEY OF CHILDHOOD.

Sweet vale, where I rambled, a reckless child,
Mid brooks and wild flowers, my spirit as wild,
Thy river, thy church-bells, still chime in my ears,
I see thy green beauty through memory's tears.

Since I quitted thy shade, no flowrets that shine,
No streamlets that glide, seem radiant as thine;
No music of art, no magic of words,
Sound sweet as thy bells, or the songs of thy birds.

The needle is far from the pole it obeys,
So my foot from thy solitude distantly strays;
But true to the North as that needle will be,
My heart, lovely valley, turns constant to thee.

Sweet vale, where I rambled, a reckless child,
Mid brooks and wild flowers, my spirit as wild,
Thy river, thy church-bells, still chime in my ears,
I see thy green beauty through memory's tears.

HAPPY MEMORIES.

HAPPY season! when a child
  Flowers I plucked of gayest dyes,
And, with laugh and footstep wild,
  Chased the bright-wing'd butterflies;
    All my heart in play,
    Gleesome all the day,
Easy conscience, careless breast—
Shall I be again so blest?

Wondering season! when I first
  Saw the round moon softly shine;
When rich music on me burst,
  O what ecstasy was mine!
    Then to ear and sight
    All things gave delight;
All things new, in glory drest—
Shall I be again so blest?

Dreaming season! when I bent
  Spell-bound first o'er fiction's page,
Passion's tale such witchery lent,
  Charming that romantic age;

Then no unbelief,
Then no real grief;
Fancies sweet my heart possessed—
Shall I be again so blest?

STAR OF GLORY.

STAR of glory sweetly beaming
On the azure brow of night!
Clouds across the sky are streaming,
But again it sparkles bright;
Time no dimness to it bringeth,
Nightly shining, shining there;
Sure some angel to it singeth,
Ever changeless, ever fair.

So my love, in life's wide heaven,
Shines for thee; let clouds of ill
O'er my troubled soul be driven,
'Tis not quenched, but shining still:
Time no single ray is stealing
From love's calm enduring light;
'Tis a star of truth and feeling,
Burning ever pure and bright.

Like that distant orb of splendour,
  Thou far off mayst wandering be,
But no distance e'er will render
  My affection dim for thee:
Radiant ever, clouds of sorrow
  Love shall lace with silvery gleams,
And no light it needs to borrow,
  In itself a fount of beams.

THE GOOD AND FAIR.

Love thou all things good and fair,
  From the mighty stars of God,
To the lark that hymns in air,
  To the flower that decks the sod:
Love will make thine eyes beam bright,
  As the eyes of angels shine;
Hatred, with a cloud, will blight
  All things beauteous and divine.

Love the infant rill that leaps
  Sparkling, laughing, under willows;
Love old ocean as he sweeps,
  With his voice of stormy billows:

Love the valley, love the mountain
  Holding converse with the sky;
Love the minnow in the fountain,
  And the insect glittering by.

Love mankind, and smile, and bless;
  Heap no evil on thy foe;
Love is peace, is happiness,
  Hate another name for woe:
Love at first from heaven descended,
  Giv'n to cheer our night of ill;
'Tis with all things beauteous blended,
  'Twould make earth an Eden still.

THE END.

www.ingramcontent.com/pod-product-compliance
Lightning Source LLC
Chambersburg PA
CBHW031028120726
47905CB00007B/2094